Praise for *Winning Your High-Conflict Divorce*

In her groundbreaking book *Winning Your High-Conflict Divorce*, author Shelly Loomus combines her mental health, legal back-ground and personal experiences, offering important strategies to divorcing parents Loomus provides a comprehensive explanation with attention to detail and rich case examples to prove her points. Readers will appreciate her use of metaphors to deepen their understanding of the unique nature of the conflicts and the importance of the ways one must respond. I highly recommend this knowledgeable, thought provoking, helpful and realistic book written from a unique perspective about winning your high-conflict divorce. The reader will not only be well-informed but left with a sense of hope and optimism.

— *Toni P. Kaplan, Ph.D., Clinical Psychologists*

Winning Your High-Conflict Divorce is a must-read for anyone wading through a challenging, messy divorce. Its explanations of the divorce process and practical advice for strategizing and coping will be invaluable to anyone struggling through the painful and emotionally scarring process of divorce. Shelly Loomus is an exceptional lawyer, therapist, and human being. She has written a practical, informative guide featuring anecdotes, explanations of the legal process, and tools for strategizing. *Winning Your High-Conflict Divorce* provides a wealth of wisdom and useful information.

— *Andrea Nitzkin, LMSW*

continued ......

Divorce under most circumstances is difficult. It is a nightmare when one spouse thrives on conflict. Shelly Loomus has written a wise, compassionate, brave, and practical guide to surviving these painful situations with one's finances, relationships with children, and dignity intact. I highly recommend her book to anyone facing the challenge of a combative divorce and to any professional who helps them.

— *Rabbi Aaron Bergman*

Endorsements

"When I met Ms. Loomus, I did not know what to expect but I was more than pleasantly surprised. She distills all her own personal and professional experience into a means that can be understood intellectually as well as emotionally. There is no substitute for a professional who has already walked a mile in your shoes."

— Daniel Menkes, MD

"I went through a very high-conflict divorce involving a multitude of challenges. The emotional toll and financial burdens were often overwhelming and confusing. I turned to Shelly Loomus, JD, MSW for advice and to help provide understanding and direction. With her dual background in social work and law, she was able to share professional knowledge and sound advice with warmth and understanding. I will always be grateful to her for providing both clarity and compassion, which I found to be tremendously helpful. With her patience and assistance, I was able to get through this difficult time."

— Shoshana Rubenstein, ACSW

WINNING
YOUR HIGH-CONFLICT
DIVORCE
Strategies for Moms and Dads

WINNING
YOUR HIGH-CONFLICT
DIVORCE
Strategies for Moms and Dads

R. Shelly Loomus, JD, MSW

Published by Manage Your Conflict, LLC

Library of Congress Control Number 2015904939

ISBN 978-0-692-41302-9

To Lon, with love and gratitude for your unwavering support.
To my children, the blessings in my life.
And to Keri, for all your time and effort.

CONTENTS

INTRODUCTION

"It is nearing the end of the millennium and my life has been reduced to a cliché. Two kids. Nice house. A forsaken career. And a husband who says that although I am a fantastic mother and he could not have built his multimillion-dollar business without me, it just isn't enough. He wants more. More love. More adoration. A fresh start without the baggage. I am the baggage."

I wrote those words in my journal over a decade ago, at the beginning of a journey that permanently altered the course of my life. When my husband walked out the door, our oldest son was 4 and my youngest was not yet a year. In my confusion, I asked him, "On a scale of one to 10, how unhappy are you?"

"Two," he answered.

"Most people would be okay with that."

He looked at me and without hesitation said, "I'm not most people."

I did not want the divorce. I did not want my children growing up in two households and I was ashamed that my marriage failed. Simultaneously I both despised my husband for breaking apart our family and I wanted him to return so we could resume our lives.

The divorce was lengthy, lasting over a decade, and high conflict. My husband hired two different law firms to fight me: one to take the children and one to take the property. During the early years, we were in litigation or mediation at least once a month. Later our conflicts erupted less frequently and the time between our clashes extended to six months or a year. I had to defend our son's right to play soccer at his elementary school (instead of at a school halfway between his father's home and mine where he knew nobody) and my right to attend those practices. I had to enforce his obligation to keep the children insured. Not every issue brought us to court or mediation. Many conflicts I managed outside of the legal system.

Although I was trained as a lawyer, I did not like fighting. I came from a family where voices were never raised and disapproval was transmitted with a look, not an open palm. But I learned. I made mistakes along the way. There were times I could have given in. There were times I should have fought smarter. But I never gave up on myself or my kids. At some point, I decided that my choices, both during the divorce and beyond, would not be reactive. I was not going to ride up and down on the roller coaster of my husband's anger. I asked myself repeatedly: What do you want? My answer was to raise my children and teach them the skills they would need so they did not end up in a marriage and divorce like mine.

I also wanted to help others; people like me, who found themselves trapped in a war born from the fragments of shattered love. I began practicing family law. I became a mediator. I discovered I had a talent for creative problem solving. And finally, I authored this book. It is a culmination of my own experiences and more than a decade working with people who have struggled to maintain control over their lives while enduring constant conflict with someone who once loved them. Some of the stories are mine. Some are from my clients. Some are stories shared by people I have met along the way. I have changed the names and genders to protect people. In my experience working with high-conflict divorces, I have found that both men and women can be the source of the conflict.

In this book, you will find strategies that have worked. My own life is a testament to their effectiveness. I am remarried. My new husband and I joke that I "won" my divorce. I "won" because with him we have created the family life I had originally wanted. My children are well adjusted and happy. And eventually, after too many years, my divorce finally ended. Only you can define what your "win" will look like. But you will not achieve it if you allow your high-conflict divorce to consume your life. At a minimum, your "win" is to take charge of your situation. With the help of this book, you can take back your life.

CHAPTER ONE:

onflict, we are told, is bad. It is damaging to all people involved, especially the children. Countless books offer advice on how to manage the conflicts in your life, but they are all based on the assumption that the person you are dealing with is rational and also wants to end the conflict. The assumption is that neither of you know how. But in a high-conflict divorce, one person *lives* for the conflict. They are energized by it. It defines them, and therefore they fight tenaciously because to lose or to give up would be tantamount to death. In a conflict with such a person, the rational approach will not work. They will not listen to "I" statements. Telling that that when they do X you feel Y merely gives them incentive to continue.

Over the years, numerous studies have examined the effects of divorce on children. The majority concur that the divorce itself is not necessarily harmful. Continued involvement of both parents in the lives of their children results in better adjustment of everyone. That is not to say divorce has no impact on children. It is well established that experiencing divorce leads to lower performance in school and enhanced social-adjustment challenges. Children who experience their parents' divorce without support are more likely to have long-term emotional and behavioral problems. The psychological damage of divorce is reduced, however, by preserving a child's relationships with both parents.

For most families this is possible. Seventy-five percent of divorced families can significantly reduce parental conflict within two to four years after the divorce is finalized. These parents learn to work together within the new family structure. They can consult with one another and agree on the children's needs. The other twenty-five percent, however, remain embroiled in conflict up to four- or five-years post-divorce, sometimes longer. Children in these families are in greater danger of long-term negative effects from their parents' divorce. Their parents' conflicts create tremendous stress for them. The more frequent the conflict, the more these children are at risk for stunted or delayed adjustment, resulting in serious behavioral and emotional problems. These children are likely to show signs of anxiety, depression, aggression, or isolation. Unresolved conflicts may also cause them to feel anger, distress, and aggressiveness. Children experiencing high-conflict divorces are two to four times more likely to be clinically disturbed, both emotionally and behaviorally, than children in so called "normal" divorces.

Ongoing conflict is also detrimental to the adults. Research confirms that the brain interprets a disruption of the family and threatened parental status as an assault. "An attack on parenthood becomes an attack on self."[1] The possibility of losing custody, financial security, or one's life partner, engages the portion of the brain wired for survival. They engage in "fight or flight" survival techniques. The body produces adrenaline, raising heart rate and respiration as it prepares to engage in battle. If that battle never ends, adrenaline remains in

---

1 Weinstein, J. & Weinstein, R., 2005, "I Know Better Than That:" The Role of Emotions and the Brain, 7 J. L. Fam. Stud. 351

the body, making it vulnerable to multiple medical complications including memory loss, weight gain and an increased risk of heart attack or stroke.[2]

Psychologically, adults subject to unrelenting stress develop depression and anxiety disorders that negatively impact their functioning at home and at work. It interferes with their ability to effectively parent their children and to move on with their lives. So why do twenty-five percent of divorced couples continue fighting long after the divorce is over? They do it because they cannot *not* do it. They cannot avoid the conflict.

WHY YOU ARE SUFFERING

Because divorce is an ending, there is loss, and with loss there is grief. People experience loss in various stages. Psychiatrist Elisabeth Kübler-Ross identified them as denial, anger, bargaining, depression and finally acceptance. Most divorcing parents work through these changing emotions and return to some semblance of normalcy within two to three years. For twenty-five to thirty percent of divorcing couples, one parent remains trapped in the anger stage. That is because as many as sixty percent of the parents entrenched in long-term family court battles are personality disordered.

The pain from the losses from divorce can be excruciating, but for a person suffering from a mental health challenge, such as a personality disorder, the pain actually feels worse. These people cannot endure any discomfort. They have no stress tolerance and no

---

2 *Id.*

willingness – or ability – to self-reflect. They are incapable of comforting themselves. That is because their pain originates from within. It derives from a lifetime of unfortunate experiences that they cannot – or will not – examine. The pain inside is the residue of the ancient voices of critical parents, teachers, and peers. It says that they have done something wrong. That they are bad. That they are unlovable. This is an intolerable voice and because it has caused them so much pain, they will forever deny it. They slam the door on it. And having done that for so long, it is now a reflex, an instantaneous response. They *will never – can never* – admit that those voices might be right, and they might be wrong. Their agony is intolerable, but rather than address it they elect instead to externalize it and experience it as anger. A personality disordered person thrives on fighting because their fight is a quest for personal validation. It is a quest to quiet those voices and prove them wrong.

Such people experience the world in black and white. You are either with them or against them. Their relationships can shift from friend to foe and back to friend again within the span of minutes. But once the divorce commences – regardless of who initiated – their ex-spouse's role in their life is solidified. Their ex-spouse becomes the enemy. Having refused to acknowledge that much of the battle comes from within and not from the behavior of their ex-spouse, they instead view their ex-spouse as evil incarnate.

This person will do anything, sacrifice everything, to win the conflict. They will exploit any negative information available to them, inflate their ex-spouse's mistakes, and lie. They will provoke and manipulate them knowing that their actions will cause a negative response that they can later extort. The more pain they can inflict, the better. They will continue to abuse their ex-spouse verbally and physically. They will litigate and re-litigate issues, not only because winning is essential to their well-being, but because litigation costs their ex-spouse money, time, and stress. Their mission is to punish their ex-spouse for the pain they caused, and their strategy is to take what their ex-spouse values most: the children. This person will not act in their children's best interests. Instead, they will sacrifice their children to win.

When faced with such an opponent who can never give up the fight because they are really fighting themself, *you cannot avoid* the conflict. Walking away is untenable because *you* are not willing to sacrifice your children. You must fight to protect your children and yourself. The advice of experts who speak of win-win strategies will not help. Their solutions are for people with an end game. In your situation, the conflict itself is the end game. You must find strategies that enable you to engage in that enduring battle without allowing that battle to consume your life.

MORE ABOUT PERSONALITY DISORDERS

According to the National Institute of Mental Health, 9.1 percent of adults suffer from a personality disorder. A person with a personality disorder exhibits behavior that deviates from social norms. They engage in black-and-white thinking, divide people into camps of all good and all bad, and view anyone who fails to agree with them as the enemy. They tend to be inflexible, rigid, and unable to respond to the changes and demands of life. While there are many types of personality disorders, two are prominent in the high-conflict divorce arena. They are *Narcissist Personality Disorder* (NPD) and *Borderline Personality Disorder* (BPD).

People suffering from BPD experience patterns of intense and stormy relationships with family, friends and loved ones, often vacillating between feelings of extreme closeness and love (idealization) to extreme dislike or anger. Such people are subject to intense and highly changeable moods. They display inappropriate, intense anger and have problems controlling that anger.

It is estimated that one percent of the population suffers from NPD. People with NPD have an exaggerated sense of self-importance. They believe they are special and have an unrelenting sense of entitlement. They require constant admiration. Significantly, people with NPD lack empathy and refuse to recognize or identify with the feelings and needs of others. Consequently, they will exploit friends and family. Their relationships are superficial and exist solely to serve themselves.

Because people with NPD have an inflated sense of self, they are unable to bear painful emotions. The slightest hint of criticism, rejection, or failure is met with disproportionate rage. This difficulty coping with loss results in NPDs having tremendous difficulty overcoming the rejection inherent in divorce. Thus, they are more likely to engage in hostile conflict with their ex-spouses.

People with personality disorders believe their behavior is normal. They have little insight, deny any contribution to their own problems, and feel justified blaming others. They are dishonest with themselves. All these behaviors aggravate the conflict with their former spouse. Unfortunately, the adversarial nature of our judicial system also encourages the conflict. Our legal system is designed for each party to present their case to win the judge's approval. It is a win-or-lose battle; and the battlefield mentality encourages parties not only to exaggerate their own case, but also to undermine their opponent's. Anything for success. A personality-disordered parent, willing to lie, exploit, and sacrifice children, is a formidable adversary. One willing to expend the financial resources to litigate and re-litigate even minor issues, is even more daunting.

Fighting back, while necessary, has the unfortunate consequence of solidifying the personality-disordered parent's hatred. Your smallest win is their loss. Entitled to everything, any loss is as unacceptable as their left fist refusing to clench. Loss amplifies their rage, as do the "lies" you share in open court. They will never acknowledge the world as you see it and will fight ceaselessly to preserve their own truths. Where once you were beloved, now you are evil. Their campaign against you becomes their noble quest.

A WORD ABOUT DOMESTIC VIOLENCE

Domestic violence, or intimate partner violence, is more than physical assault. It is a pattern of abusive behavior used to gain or maintain power and control over a spouse or intimate partner. This occurs through fear and intimidation as well as the threat or use of violence. Not all forms of domestic violence include physical assault. Most domestic partner abuse consists of humiliating, isolating, terrorizing, blaming, name-calling, making the partner feel they are crazy, creating fear, and controlling money.

Perpetrators of domestic violence also use the children as vehicles for abuse. They fight for custody or a greater share of parenting time. They actively work to damage a partner's relationship with their children. They use visitation to harass their ex-spouse. They use children to deliver messages. And they deny their children, or hurt their children, knowing that they will hurt their partner-victim too.

Batterers are most commonly male, but perpetrators of domestic violence are also women.

Many batterers do not have a diagnosable mental health condition. Many do. But battering happens when one person believes they are entitled to control another. This behavior may be learned from a family of origin or culture. Regardless, when domestic violence was present in the marriage, it will be present in the divorce. The divorce *will* be high conflict.

The most dangerous time for a victim of domestic violence is when they attempt to leave or when they file for divorce. It may take years before the victim is able to disengage from the relationship. If there are minor children involved, there will be *some* ongoing interaction until the youngest child reaches the age of 18. During that time, the abuse can continue or escalate.

If you are fearful for the physical safety of yourself or your children, it is imperative that you plan carefully before filing a complaint for divorce. Having an escape plan to keep you and your children safe is critical. There are local and national resources available.[3] But this is not a book about protecting yourself from physical assault. This book focuses on victims of emotional and mental abuse who are attempting to disengage from their abuser through the legal

---

3 See National Coalition Against Domestic Violence at http://www.ncadv.org/.

system. It is written to help those people maneuver through the legal system and recover their lives.

HOW THEY DO IT

The defining characteristic of a personality-disordered person, particularly narcissists, is that they cannot see the world from any viewpoint other than their own. *They* are the only person in the world and your sole value is in how you can serve them. They are the Leading Actor, and you are the Supporting Actor in the "movie" that is their life. And to manipulate you into willingly assuming that role, the personality-disordered narcissist understands they cannot always act "larger than life." They must be craftier.

How does the narcissist convince you to relinquish your role as "Leading Actor" in your own life and be the "Sidekick" in theirs? One way is to exploit your compassion. The narcissist understands that most people believe in fairness. If the narcissist is a victim of unfairness, you are likely to come to their aid. You will help fight their battle, or perhaps fight it for them. One woman I know was always a "victim of sexism." She was the only female engineer at the company where she worked, and she confided in her new daughter-in-law how sexist her male bosses were and how poorly they treated her. The young woman was overjoyed that her mother-in-law confided in her. She was naturally sympathetic to the older woman's plight, and they bonded over the narrow-mindedness of men in the workplace. This young woman gave up hours of her time listening to her mother-in-law, offering support and advice and, even at times, helping her draft letters of protest. She once missed an entire day of work waiting at her mother-in-law's house for a delivery, agreeing it was "fairer" for her to miss a day at her own job because her mother-in-law's employers were "crueler" than hers. By being compassionate to her narcissist mother-in-law's "plight," the daughter-in-law subordinated her own needs for her mother-in-law's. It was only years later that the younger woman understood that the bosses did not treat her mother-in-law poorly because she was a woman, but because she was unstable. In fact, it is to their credit that they retained her despite all the trouble she caused them.

Another way the narcissist engages you is by playing "dumb." The narcissist will purposely do something they know will anger you but cover it up by acting as if they simply did not understand. Suppose, for example, you are divorced and have a court order requiring your ex-spouse to provide you with an itinerary when they take the children on vacation. Your narcissist ex arrives at the door having "forgotten" or "not understanding" what they were supposed to do. "Sorry," they say and appear bashful so that you feel silly demanding that they follow the rules. Or perhaps they only give you partial information. Maybe the flight number or the name of the hotel is missing. Should you complain, they deride *you*. They might say that you have their cell phone number (even though they never answer your call) or that you could "look it up yourself." They will be defensive, acting as if they simply "made a mistake" and you are being intolerant. "That's what's wrong with you," they might say. "You always have to be perfect."

Even more calculating is the narcissist who asks you to explain. You willingly help them understand you, hoping they will become more considerate. But that is not their true motive. Instead, they are looking for a vulnerable place to attack. I know one man who tried scheduling a family event with his brother. This man had children involved in multiple activities, whereas the brother was single. Before they spoke, the man and his wife went through the family calendar to identify possible dates. When he presented the dates to his brother, the brother tentatively agreed to one despite its "inconvenience," and then began asking about the unavailable dates. "Why won't this one work?" and "Why won't that one work?" he demanded. The man painstakingly explained each scheduling conflict as the brother's questions became more focused and hostile. Eventually, the brother accused the man of "thinking only of himself," repeating a lifelong grudge and reinforcing his view of the world that he was the "good brother," and the man was the "selfish brother."

Whatever tactic the narcissist chooses, the goal is to keep you in servitude. You are constantly trying to prove that you are not selfish or intolerant, but that you are helpful and supportive. You give up your time, perhaps your children's soccer game, or even your concern about where your children might be traveling, to make your point, believing that you are building a relationship. But, in reality, you are being manipulated into once again acting as the expendable sidekick in the movie that stars the narcissist.

The narcissist ensnares you by making you the center of their world for a brief time. Their agenda is hurried because taking too long to snare you risks you discovering the truth.

They are charming and know how to market themselves. They excel at it. Certainly, you would never have consented to that first date if they were not. The trouble is that they believe their own public relations and acts so sincerely that others believe them, too. It is important because, by validating their **Public Persona**, they can continue denying the demon within.

When you married, you, too, accepted your spouse's Public Persona. But when you divorced, you divorced the real person. It is natural to want to expose that real person, to want to be validated. Close friends and family may understand, and perhaps some people you have met along the way, but most who encounter your former spouse for only a brief period, such as the judge in your case, will not. This is because your former spouse is skilled at creating that Public Persona. They have spent a lifetime perfecting it and are an expert of the **Appearance Game.**

Your former spouse is a thespian. They understand how to exploit people by appearing to give them what they want, and they are willing to do so. Lying is a tool. Something useful to help them win the prize. In a divorce, the prize is the children and the property. To attain them, the narcissist will be ruthless. But they will not always be overt. Their skill is in their subtlety and apparent sincerity. Your former spouse will stand before the judge and profess their undying love for their children. They are believable because they believe it themselves. Even if the day before they slapped your daughter for forgetting to put her plate in the dishwasher, by the time they are in court, they will have forgotten that event. They will appear to be a parent who genuinely loves their child and wants to spend time with them.

If you try telling the judge your truth, that your daughter cried for three hours – not from the physical pain but from the emotional hurt – you will not succeed. Your personality-disordered former spouse will instantly rewrite history and have a valid excuse for their behavior. They may even blame you, and ultimately you will look foolish while they appear innocent. They are chameleons and are far better at charming the judge than you are.

There is one other risk in trying to expose your former spouse. Once they understand what you are trying to do, they *will* use it against you. They will deviously bait you because they *want* you to continue seeking validation from the judge. They want you to complain to the judge about all the terrible things they have done, confident that they will successfully refute your allegations. They do this not only so you look foolish, but also because they understand that the more you complain to the judge, the more you appear to be alienating them from their children. Standing in court and sincerely proclaiming their love for their children while you whine about their behavior will give them their win.

KNOWING THE TRICKS OF THEIR TRADE

In high-conflict divorces, personality-disordered parents use tactics that have proven effective. They bully, abuse, and litigate. They provoke and manipulate. After they separated, Gary broke through a locked door, pinned his wife against the wall and yelled at her continually until she finally relented to his demands. When she later asked how he could do such a thing, he smiled smugly and said, "I did it because it worked." And it was true. Tyrants torment because it works. To defend yourself against your tyrannical ex-spouse, you must know the tactics they use and *how* to effectively deflect them.

Lies and Personal Attacks

A personality-disordered person thrives on fighting. Because they see themselves as either superior to others or a victim of others, every fight is a quest for personal validation. Whatever the subject of the conflict, they fight to prove their entitlement. Because they are better than you. Or to prove that you are *not* better than them. For them, every fight is a holy war.

Of course, these motives are subconscious. They do not realize that the real struggle is within, which explains why the conflict will never end. Until they vanquish the demons within, they will project those demons onto you. You are an easy target.

There are no scruples in a holy war. If your former spouse is a victim, then you are the Evil Oppressor. That label makes you fair game for personal attack. Gary accused his ex-wife of being an incompetent mother. He worked fourteen-hour days building his marketing business but wrote in a court document that he "honestly didn't know how his wife could care for the children without his help." A man I know named David was accused of being an incompetent father because he wanted to take the children on a Royal Caribbean cruise. His ex-wife's attorney, a father himself, argued that "fathers notoriously make bad decisions." David's ex-wife also complained to the judge, in another hearing, that he had told their sons to call his new wife "Mommy." David did not do that, although *she* had told them to call *her* new husband "Daddy."

A personality-disordered person believes their lies. Their defense mechanisms are so finely tuned that the minute the words are spoken they become truth. They are experts at revising history, and they believe their new reality so sincerely that they sound sincere.

The lies and personal attacks are hurtful, but they offer insight into your ex-spouse's mind. Somewhere within the deep recesses of his mind, Gary understood he was a neglectful parent. But he was unable to face that reality, so he projected his truth onto his ex-wife.

Projection is a psychological concept developed by the renowned psychiatrist Dr. Sigmund Freud. It occurs when someone unconsciously ascribes their own unacceptable personality traits to another. It is natural to want to defend yourself and to explain that the *actual* negligent parent is the accuser, your ex-spouse. But this is a trap designed to bait you and you must work carefully to avoid it.

Your calculating ex-spouse knows you well and if they can deflect the conversation away from the *real* issue – in David's case acquiring a court order allowing him to take the children on vacation – then they have a greater chance of winning. Time is limited and if it is consumed by insults – defenses – and counter-insults (mudslinging), there is less time to focus on substance. Second, you risk appearing defensive and there is a tendency to believe that defensive people are guilty. If you protest too much, people suspect there must be some truth to the accusation.

And finally, family law judges' patience with mudslinging is remarkably small. They hear it every day – all day. They do not want to rule on a "he-said-she-said" argument that has no bearing on the legal issues. If you defend yourself from the lies, you risk the judge getting angry. And when judges get angry, they often punish both parties. If you do not allow some lies to linger unrefuted, then you risk losing the larger issue. The personality-disordered person understands the power of the personal attack.

Another battle strategy is to "up the ante." This was how the U.S.

brought down the Soviet Union in the 1980s. By accelerating the arms race to unattainable levels, the Soviets faced a choice of financial implosion or defeat. For a personality-disordered person whose objective is to perpetuate the conflict, raising the stakes is a logical approach. After Sarah and her husband divorced, he remarried a Christian woman. Sarah continued raising their son in the Jewish faith. When it was time for his bar mitzvah, she selected a date and let her former husband know. Even though he was no longer practicing Judaism and had agreed that all religious holidays would be on her parenting time, he took her to court and asked the judge to punish her for excluding him. In her response, Sarah noted that he had abandoned Judaism, to which he "upped the ante" by asking the judge to give him parenting time for half of the religious holidays he had previously relinquished. He sought far more than he had originally requested because once battle began and she challenged his truth, he *needed* to regain everything she had taken from him. In his mind, he never abandoned his religion and was *entitled* to half of the holidays. If questioned, he would deny he ever willingly gave them up.

I grew up in a world where truth was intrinsic. I believed justice would prevail when the truth was disclosed. But I learned that disordered people believe each revision of history they construct, and I have witnessed them deliver their narratives with such sincerity that sometimes even their ex-spouses doubted their own truths. Events that occur behind closed doors, with only two people present, are subject to interpretation. No one lives with sinister theme music playing in the background to alert us to evil. We have only our instincts, which can be subject to doubt.

If you say, "You offended me," and they deny it, arguing that you are too sensitive, who would be right? What is the truth? You gut might tell you that their words were hurtful, but when the story is later recounted, their conviction in their tale will be immutable. How do you resolve a conflict rooted in self-deception?

Be prepared for your former spouse to lie with impunity. I know one man who claimed his wife physically abused him after he had put *her* in the hospital for injuries *he* had caused. Some assertions contain just enough accuracy to ring true. Gary sought more parenting time. He emphasized his happy home life, even displayed pictures of himself and his children, his wife, and stepchildren, smiling and hugging one another. He spoke about how important it was for the children to remain part of that family experience. He won, but within three months, he and his wife separated and later divorced. How much truth was there in his claim? Enough. The truth can be manipulated, and reality in a courtroom is only what the judge chooses to believe.

Frequently Litigating

Frequent litigation is a commonly used tactic to drive up your expenses, consume your time, and add tremendous stress to your life. Recurrent litigation is both financially and emotionally exhausting. A divorce commonly costs anywhere from $10,000 to $35,000. The cost of court fees for a two-day trial can run as much as $25,000. But these are not high-conflict cases that generate multiple court appearances. One study concluded that nearly a quarter of battered mothers in contested custody disputes are driven into bankruptcy after being forced to pay enormous fees for lawyers, mediators, custody evaluators and parent coordinators.

Frequent litigation also drains away time you could be spending with your children or at work or with your friends. I know of a man who always filed his motions just as his ex-wife's parenting time began. She was forced to choose to either work on her response – rather than be with her children – or delay responding to focus on her family, a challenging task with the stress of another impending court appearance hovering in the shadows. Frequent litigation keeps you on the defensive and feeling like a caged animal.

Personality-disordered people are expert manipulators. They know how to provoke their ex-spouses into behaving aggressively or even violently. Their attacks are sly and without witnesses, but their ex-spouse's response may be very public. A personality-disordered ex-spouse might make suggestions that cause their ex-spouse to reasonably fear they will kidnap the children, for example. Their words or actions will be subtle, but the ex-spouse will know what message they are conveying. As a result, the ex might withhold the children or flee to protect them. If there is no documentation to substantiate the ex's concerns, they will be punished. Meanwhile, the personality-disordered person appears pure and innocent.

The most common focus of the litigation is custody of the children. Personality-disordered ex-spouses feel entitled to custody of their children. They also intuitively understand that gaining custody will devastate you – an added benefit. Court aggravates this conflict because to win custody in our adversarial system, parents are forced to publicly discredit one another. Each parent must prove to the judge that awarding them custody is in the best interests of the children. At a minimum, this requires each parent to highlight their positive traits while inflating the other's negative traits.

Personality-disordered parents fight unscrupulously and drag you into the mud with them. Once you have engaged in that battle, there is no recovery. By insulting your personality-disordered ex-spouse you have confirmed every evil trait they had ascribed to you, further solidifying their resolve.

Court also offers opportunities to perpetuate the conflict. Dragging out court actions by asking for **continuances** (delays) buys time. When asked for, your attorney, who is a member of the family law bar of your state, will agree as a courtesy. Delays are not only time consuming, but costly. Your attorney must prepare for each hearing. If the hearing is delayed for two weeks, they will have to prepare again. They charge by the hour, and you will have paid twice for the same preparation.

Furthermore, in high-conflict cases, disturbing events frequently occur. Within that two-week delay, it is possible for a new conflict to arise. In that case, your attorney will have to spend time (and your money) preparing to address that issue as well. Finally, extra time gives your industrious ex-spouse more opportunities to work against you. I know of one man who used his additional two weeks to gather affidavits supporting his assertion that he deserved custody, and his ex-wife did not.

On the other side, your former spouse may try to rush you to settle your case. In this strategy, they offer you a fraction of what you are legally entitled to, threatening more litigation if you do not agree. They may say, for example, that they are being "reasonable" now, but if you do not agree to their offer, they will go to trial and seek full custody of the children. Or they may offer you a package deal. Legally, issues of custody, parenting time, support, and property division are resolved separately. Custody, for example, cannot be given in exchange for property. But your personality-disordered former spouse may present you with an offer that bundles everything together, again threatening to demand much more if you do not agree.

The appeal of having it "over and done with" can be tempting. But if you agree to the "take it or leave it" package presented to you, your personality-disordered former spouse learns that, with enough pressure, you will relent. You can be certain they will re-use this successful trick.

Limiting Your Parenting Time

Because you have legal rights to your personality-disordered ex-spouse's property, their assets, their income, and *their* children, they are resolved to regain control. They have many tools at their disposal. The most obvious way to retain control and punish you is by eliminating you rights to the children. If they cannot gain custody, they may engage authorities (Child Protective Services or the police) to take the children from you by filing false claims. Heather accused her ex-husband of kidnapping their children even though she knew exactly where they were and, moments before she filed the police report, she had spoken to her son on Facebook. When the police failed to charge the father, she enlisted her attorney to file a motion asking the judge to punish him. Interestingly, she did not request make-up parenting time. She simply wanted the judge to validate her reality that her ex-husband "kidnapped" the children. The judge refused, and she lost.

A less obvious but more effective tactic is complaining to the judge that you are exploiting their orders. Judges become angry if they believe their orders are being disregarded. This strategy is effective because disproving the claim is difficult. It is their word against yours. In another attempt to limit her ex-husband's parenting time, Heather argued that her former husband should not attend their child's Little League games. She told the judge that when he attended games scheduled on *her* parenting time, he dominated the child's attention and distracted him from the game. In another instance, Chris complained to the judge that when his former wife called the children on the telephone, she monopolized their time for hours, preventing them from finishing their homework. He inflated that reality and denied that when the children were on the phone with their mother it was because *she* was the parent who helped them with their math and listened to their problems. Later, Chris took the children on a cruise and locked their cell phones in the safe, telling them the calls were too expensive. What their children did not know was that their mother paid the cell-phone charges and she had specifically told Chris she would pay for the long-distance calls. Obviously, saving her money was not his concern. Interfering with her relationship with the children was.

Despite their vapid sincerity, your former spouse's pursuit of custody or more parenting time is often more about limiting your time than any actual desire to be with their children. When they demand more time or try to limit yours, it is not because they want to spend time with the children. The children are accessories they want under their roof, whether they "wear" them or not. The newspaper is filled with countless stories of parents leaving their children. I know many parents who, once the kids are with them, ignore them. They spend extra hours at work or go shopping or sit in front of the television or computer. Maryanne and her husband left her children in a van for hours during a New Year's Eve party. Her ex-husband offered to keep them at home with him but, because it was her parenting time, she refused. Emma argued to the judge that her ex-husband should not attend his children's soccer games when they occurred on *her* parenting time. And Chris refused to allow his ex-wife to hold their infant son even though the baby was reaching for her and crying. With personality-disordered ex-spouses, it is rarely about the kids.

Hurting You by Hurting the Children

Personality-disordered parents will hurt your children because they know that hurting them hurts you. They make horrible, some-times dangerous, parenting choices that terrify you but are not il-legal. Thus, you have no grounds to have them arrested. Barry and his new wife took the children on vacation to Mexico for a week. They rented two cottages on the Resort property. Barry and his wife stayed in one and the children, ages eleven and eight, stayed alone in the other. This happened around the time four-year-old Madeleine McCann was abducted from her hotel room in Portugal. Barry's for-mer wife was furious at the sleeping arrangements but was helpless to do anything about it.

On another occasion, Barry allowed the two young boys to go to the bathroom and concession stand alone during half-time at a pro-fessional sport's game. The arena was in the middle of a major city and seated 18,000 people. The children were gone for 45 minutes while Barry chatted on his cell phone. They could have been abducted and gone long before Barry noticed. But what he did was not illegal, although it terrified his ex-wife. Even had the police investigated,

Barry would have skillfully denied any wrongdoing. Nor would the court accept the young children's words as truth, dismissing them as unreliable or manipulative.

You want your children to be safe and happy. You want your children to have the best that you can give them. Most parents do, enrolling them in extracurricular activities that are fun and important for proper development. But personality-disordered parents often refuse to allow the children to participate in activities that occur during *their* parenting time. They claim their ex-spouse has no legal right to interfere with their parenting time, that they are too busy, or the activity is not appropriate.

Unable to fully participate, perhaps only attending dance class on mom's time, the child has a higher chance of failing. Sarah's former husband, for example, refused to take their son to Taekwondo on *his* Saturdays. Because the boy could only go to half of the classes, he did not advance as quickly as his friends. He fell behind and became discouraged. Eventually he quit. This hurt Sarah because she knew her son loved the activity, and she believed it would improve his self-esteem. His father's decision damaged it instead.

You know what your children want but have no control over their time when they are with their other parent. This is frustrating and often painful, and your personality-disordered former spouse revels in that.

David was the parent who *heard* his twelve-year-old daughter when she complained she was never allowed to go to sleepovers at her friends' houses. When he spoke to his former wife, she told him *she* was in charge during her parenting time and the sleepover was inconvenient. He offered to drive their daughter to and from the sleepover and to pay for the movie and pizza. Still, she refused. Again, this was not about convenience but about control. David's former wife was willing to deny her daughter because she could, with the added benefit that doing so hurt David as well.

Equally unscrupulous is the parent who initially agrees to an activity, only to renege later. Sarah's children were enrolled in religious school on Monday and Wednesday afternoons and Sunday mornings. Alternatively, the children could attend only on Sundays. Her oldest son enjoyed the three-day program, but Sarah's work schedule did not allow her to get him to religious school on Mondays. Her former husband agreed that the boy should continue weekday religious school and for a year he left work early, picked the children up from after-school care, drove them to religious school at 4:00 p.m. and then returned them to Sarah's house at 6:30 that evening.

When Sarah remarried, her ex-husband became angry. To punish her, he chose to renege on the Monday arrangement. He agreed that he would continue retrieving the children from religious school and return them to Sarah's house at 6:30 p.m. (which Sarah could do herself) but he would no longer collect them from after-school care and deliver them *to* religious school at 4:00 p.m. Nor would he continue Wednesday religious school, which was on *his* parenting time. Sarah knew their verbal agreement would not hold up in court. Unable to make alternative arrangements, she was forced to withdraw the children from weekday religious school. This was particularly difficult because her oldest son was preparing for his bar mitzvah, had many friends at the school, participated in the youth group there, and genuinely enjoyed the activity. None of this mattered to his father, however. He willingly hurt his son to punish Sarah.

Less overt but more insidious is the passive-aggressive parent who agrees to an activity but fails to support it. This parent is always late dropping the child off or picking them up. This parent talks on their cell phone during the entire dance recital. Or they run to Starbucks for a latte during the 45-minute Taekwondo exhibition, promising to be "right back" but returning just as it ends. This hurts the child who is fully aware of their parent's disinterest, which in turn, hurts you.

Finally, there is the parent who refuses to pay their fair share. When Barry and his wife divorced, their daughter had been taking swimming lessons. In this program, one session rolled into the next. There was no need to re-enroll. When the bill for the new session arrived, Barry refused to pay his share.

"Don't you believe she needs to learn to swim?" his ex-wife asked.

"Yes," he agreed, "but you didn't ask me first."

Barry knew it was important to his ex-wife that their daughter learn to swim. He knew that because she believed it was important, she would pay if he did not. He was right. His ex-wife reasoned that it was less costly to pay for the lessons herself than to sue him for his share. Barry had a win-win. He could control his ex-wife by demanding she get his pre-approval for any activity their daughter participated in, and that if he refused to pay, she would pay herself. Barry was in control.

Another way to control a child is by treating them as if he were too young or too old. The parent who refuses to allow their 16-year-old child to drive, claiming they are not ready while refusing to teach them, is controlling the child by belittling them. The parent who refuses to get up in the morning and take the child to school, forcing the child to keep trying to wake them up, is controlling the child by

parentifying them (making the child assume adult responsibilities). Gary did the same thing to his daughter. He consistently refused to get out of bed on schooldays. His daughter was forced to make breakfast and lunch for herself and her younger brother, all while repeatedly trying to get Gary out of bed. One day the daughter called her mother and complained that they were late to school because it had snowed during the night, and she had not realized that would slow traffic. She was only fourteen. Yet when she turned fifteen and got her driver's permit, Gary refused to let her drive, telling her she was too young and immature. This, too, is control.

Personality-disordered people are devious and practiced at using your weaknesses against you. In high-conflict divorces, the children are one person's weakness and the other's instrument of choice. If you want your child to have swimming lessons or join her friends at a sleepover, they deny the children because doing so hurts you. These parents need to remind you (and themselves) that they control the property – the children.

The children, like people everywhere, are hard-wired to want their parent's love. It is easy for a personality-disordered parent to manipulate their offspring. They say things like "I miss you when you are at your friend's house" or "I'm sad that you prefer going to camp than spending the week with me." Younger children are especially vulnerable to these claims. They do not see that once they have agreed not to go to their friend's house, this parent spends all their time on the computer, and they are left to the care of the television. They do not yet recognize that their parent's words are inconsistent with their actions.

This inconsistency is another deliberate activity that effectively controls the children. You probably recognize it from when you and your spouse were married. Changing plans at the last minute is a common control-tactic. When David's ex-wife refused to allow her daughter to go to the sleepover, she said, "We have so little time together. Don't you want to spend it with me?" The daughter agreed to stay home, and they spent 15 minutes playing a board game before the mother went off to her room and closed the door. Had the daughter complained, her mother would have made her feel guilty, accusing her of being unappreciative. This child learned not to complain so she could receive the occasional tidbit of her mother's love. She conforms to whatever mother asks hoping she will please mother and receive that token tidbit. But what is required to please a personality disordered parent changes all the time. They are unpredictable. And their love may be withdrawn at the least provocation. The child, like the ex-spouse, learns to tread lightly, always monitoring how the personality-disordered parent will respond.

The personality-disordered person controls their children and their spouse by using their emotions as a tool. They will give and take away their love and display their anger randomly. Without knowing the *rules*, family is always left guessing. This puts the personality-disordered person in control. It also keeps them the center of attention because their family is always monitoring their moods for guidance and never knowing how they will respond.

Unpredictability is a powerful tool. By saying "yes" just enough, the personality-disordered parent keeps both you and your child hoping. If they said "no" all the time, both of you would stop asking. If they were always unloving, your child would begin to hate them. But if there are enough moments of genuine love, your child will cling to the hope that there will be more. And if there is hope, the personality-disordered parent remains in control.

Damaging Your Relationship with Your Children

Regardless of the court orders that prohibit one parent from making disparaging comments about another, it happens. Again, it may not be overt. Your former spouse may not call you names in front of the children, but they will find ways to discredit you. If, for example, your child tells his father that he was punished for swearing, dad might agree that the mother is being ridiculous or overly strict. By sympathizing with his son, dad simultaneously disparages mom and creates an alliance against her.

Dad might go further by encouraging the child to swear, knowing it irritates his ex-wife. He may deliberately permit the son to do other things that his ex-wife will not approve of. Perhaps he allows his son to miss school or stay up late playing video games. Perhaps they play video games together until 2 in the morning on a school night. Not only does he undermine the mother's authority, but he also conveys to his son that they are friends while mom is an unreasonable disciplinarian. Dad might even tell his son he does not have to listen to his mother. While that may feel liberating for a child, it also creates uncertainty as he fails to learn when to honor authority. Instead of learning critical thinking skills, the child learns to reject all authority, which will cause problems for him both within and outside of his home.

Another way a parent might undermine the other parent's relationship with their children is to suggest they are unsafe. When Barry's daughter was at her mother's house, he would call to make certain she was safe. Even if she felt comfortable, he sent the message that there might be a time when she is not safe. He created doubt and uncertainty. Heather prevented her children from sitting with or even greeting their father at school functions. If this did not teach them that their father was a pariah, it certainly sent the message that they lived in two separate worlds that should *never* intersect. When her children once defied her and *did* say hello to their father after a band concert, Heather punished them for breaking the rules. She told them that it was *her* parenting time and that they and their father had violated the judge's order. If the judge found out, he would be angry, she said. Not only did she terrorize the children, but she sent a clear message that their father was a criminal for breaking the law.

By creating rules, a personality-disordered parent maintains control. They may enforce them or create new rules. They may also, on occasion, break them so their children see them as benevolent. Often the rules are capricious, and the children never know when they are violating one. Rules can appear out of thin air. Rules can disappear. Rules can have double standards, applying to the children but not to their parent. Or to one sibling but not another. Magical rules keep the children vigilant and in a perpetual state of uncertainty.

By making rules and punishing the children for violating them, a parent also has an opportunity to insert themselves into your home. They may ask that you continue punishing the children when they are with you. If the child lost television privileges for three weeks, for example, the personality-disordered parent may ask you to prohibit your child from watching television because "it is important to be consistent." They will explain that it is important to "co-parent."

While you may feel that the punishment was too harsh or the crime insignificant, you may also feel tempted to agree because consistency and co-parenting are important. The result is that you have allowed the other parent to control what happens in your house. Now the children learn that the other parent controls what occurs in both parents' houses, that the other parent is ultimately in control, and that you are not. While co-parenting and consistency are important, if there is no reciprocity, if the other parent fails to implement punishments that you impose, then the words are merely tools for gaining control.

Exploiting Flexible Parenting Plans

Inconsistency enables personality-disordered ex-spouses to retain control. If your parenting plan is flexible, your former spouse will use that to their advantage. Initially, if they have physical custody, they are likely to promise you unlimited access to your children. You believe you will see your children whenever you want. But by agreeing, you have allowed the other parent to be the gatekeeper to your children. They can grant you access or not, depending on their whim. Or depending on what you might have done recently that displeases them.

Unless the plan is extremely specific, your former spouse might frequently change the schedule, claiming the children are busy or ill. On the reverse side, a flexible plan allows your personality-disordered ex-spouse who does not have custody to use their parenting time to harass you. They may cancel at the last minute, ruining whatever your plans were that did not involve the children. Or they might arrive extremely late, which has the same result. They may fail to inform you of their visit until moments before arriving. If the children are not available, they are likely to blame you. Or they may refuse to tell you when they are returning the children. Perhaps they say they will bring the children home at 8:00 p.m. but then do not arrive until 10:00 p.m. Or on the other side, they return the children after only an hour of visitation. All these tricks prevent you from making definitive plans. Their reward is knowing they have disrupted and destabilized your life.

Enlisting Authorities

Enlisting help from outside authorities is a common tactic used in high-conflict divorces. Calling the police or Child Protective Services (CPS) and reporting that you abused your children is a tool the personality-disordered parent may use. It does not matter that the children are okay, or that the disruption of a police or CPS investigation will scare them. The children are expendable in the quest to win. Accusations are easy to make but difficult to disprove.

STEPPING UP TO THE PLATE

Living with a disordered spouse often causes you to suppress your feelings to keep the peace. After a while, you might become so numb you do not even recognize your feelings. Cheryl had planned a romantic night at a hotel for her husband's birthday. The morning they were to leave, he took his time getting ready. He delayed and delayed. As she watched the hours slip away, she saw their opportunity to take advantage of the hotel's amenities disappear. No spa. No couple's massage. She became stressed which, in turn, liberated his rage.

If she were going to be unpleasant, he said, he would not go at all. Of course, Cheryl brought herself under control, shoved her anger and disappointment under the mental rug, and was grateful when he was finally ready to leave. Her husband got what every narcissist wants. Cheryl was grateful when he finally chose to grace her with his presence.

When Cheryl's husband finally told her he wanted a divorce, she was shocked. Looking back there had been warning signs, but she had ignored them. Living with a narcissist requires total subordination of self. Because her husband had no respect for her and constantly belittled her, Cheryl had learned to suppress the voices in her head. To live with him she had to accept the world as he saw it. In that world, her feelings were irrelevant. Eventually, her inner voice was silenced. Warning signs might have been shouting in her ears, but she could no longer hear them.

Living with a narcissist, you *must* look at the world through their eyes. They will not tolerate anything else and will manipulate the situation until you do. It is tremendously difficult to take back your perspective, to see your world as it really is. It is a painful process, too, when you realize just how much of yourself you have given up keeping the peace.

Sadly, peace is almost impossible when you divorce a narcissist. They will not tolerate the rejection (even if they initiated the divorce) or the loss, and you are now their enemy. As difficult as it will be, you *must accept your reality.* You must accept that your former spouse is waging a war against you. Unless you are willing to give up everything, custody of the children and all the property, you have no choice but to fight.

You will waste time and energy trying to evade and avoid this truth. Heather's husband confessed to me that he was tired of fighting her. He spent too much energy psyching himself up each time she made a new demand or filed an action in court.

Instead of mentally sitting in the batter's box, I suggested he accept that he *lives on the plate.* "You will waste more energy 'running from the batter's box to the plate,'" I advised, "than accepting that for the time being, your life is on the plate – bat in hand – ready to swing."

Once he accepted his reality, Heather's husband was better able to strategize on how best to regain control of his life. He reduced the time and energy he spent *reacting* to Heather and became *proactive* instead. Now their children live with him.

Your war is a chess game. There will be many skirmishes and battles along the way. Sometimes you will be able to circumvent them and sometimes you will have to fight. The key is to fight smart. Know when to sacrifice a pawn to capture a rook. Know that you cannot leave the chess game until you win. Have an idea of what your win will look like. And know in your heart that you *can* win.

CHAPTER TWO:

The American judicial system is adversarial, the courtroom is the battlefield. The structure is designed to pit one person against another with the promise that justice will prevail. One person wins and the other loses. But divorce is not like other areas of law. Even if you win, you can still lose. Unlike contract law or the laws of personal injury, where once the final judgment is entered the parties walk away and never interact again, in a divorce with minor children, you and your former spouse remain connected until your youngest child turns eighteen. Sometimes longer, as there are college graduations, weddings, and other life-cycle events that offer opportunities to engage. It can be exceedingly difficult to recover from a very public dispute where all your faults and mistakes were publicly aired. The battles you fought solidify the adversarial nature of your relationship with your former spouse. For many – especially personality-disordered black-and-white thinkers – there is no going back. You have validated their belief that you are the devil, and they are committed to their new holy war; a war that may last decades.

The problem with the family law court system is that this war – your new reality – is completely contrary to the prevailing philosophy that parents should get along for the sake of their children. Our society believes children are entitled to a relationship with both their parents, and multiple studies have shown that they adjust better to their parent's divorce when they have regular and continuing contact with both. Judges *want* parents to work together. If not, they get angry.

Your personality-disordered former spouse is highly attuned to this paradigm. They learn quickly what others, including the judge in your case, wants, and their campaign against you will become increasingly sophisticated as their learning curve increases.

TRUTH IS WHAT THE JUDGE SAYS IS TRUE

There are three parties in your divorce: you, your former spouse, and the judge. The judge has ultimate control and truth is only what they hear and accept. You must tell your story in a way the judge is willing to hear.

You have three ways of communicating to the judge in your case. You or your attorney will draft legal **pleadings** – motions and briefs – outlining the law. The goal is to convince the judge that the law is on your side. You can also give the judge an **affidavit**, a sworn statement telling your story. Finally, during oral argument, you or your attorney speak to the judge and answer their questions.

It is extremely difficult to distill your complicated life story into a few persuasive pages and minutes. Too much detail and your audience – the judge – gets lost. Too little detail and they do not understand.

Your personality-disordered former spouse has the same courtroom tools you have, but they will use them differently. "Under oath" does not mean the same to them because their "truths" will change as needed.

will revise history into a new reality and sincerely believe that reality[4] – even if it has no similarity to the reality you know. Your former spouse will stand before the judge and profess their undying love for their children. They are believable because they believe it themselves. Even if they recently prevented your child from going to camp with their friends, your personality-disordered former spouse will instantly re-write history and have a valid excuse for their behavior. They may even blame you.

In his affidavit, Gary declared that he was home for dinner every night. Yes, he came home at night. And yes, he probably ate something. But that was at one or two in the morning. He did not partake in the "family dinner," as he testified. Unfortunately, there was only his wife's word against his. What was the "real truth?" Whatever the judge decided.

It is exceedingly difficult to convince the judge of your truth. It is also practically impossible to protect your children from their emotionally abusive parent through the legal system. The belief that children are entitled to a relationship with both parents is too deeply entrenched. Only when the judge believes that your former spouse might pose a physical danger to your children will they be inclined to reduce your ex-spouse's parental rights. The emotional damage your former spouse inflicts on your children will not suffice.

If you try to expose the monster that is your former spouse, not only are you likely to fail, but your efforts may backfire. The judge is likely to see your efforts to discredit your ex-spouse as a thinly

---

4 My family joke about this now. When we disagree with someone we say, "I deny your reality and substitute my own," acknowledging that in some circumstances, reality is what you believe it to be.

disguised attempt to reduce their parenting time. The judge will see *you* as the alienating parent. You may also develop a reputation in court as overprotective and neurotic, especially if your children's other parent is standing in court begging for more time with their beloved children. They are likely to get it and you may end up appearing angry and vindictive, which then dilutes your credibility with the judge.

Although judges are educated about domestic violence/intimate partner violence, some judges are simply blind to it. I represented a woman whose husband, an attorney, was without a doubt the power broker in their relationship. They had a long-term marriage, and when I met her, she presented as very uncertain and insecure. During a pretrial conference, the judge ordered the parties to mediation. I argued that it was not the best choice for my client but was restrained from using the words "domestic violence" because I was suspicious of her husband's attorney's relationship with the judge. They had spent much of the time discussing their golf outings. The judge ignored my argument and demanded that the parties mediate. Thus, parties end up in mediation even if it is not the right place for them.

One reason a judge might be unaware of your abusive situation is because they see only a snapshot of you and your ex-spouse. Abusers deliberately provoke and manipulate their partners until they react violently or aggressively. It is the reaction that the judge sees. The judge *does not care why* you reacted or behaved as you did. They do not have the time to listen to your lengthy explanation. The judge's concern is resolving the issue. If the judge sees you as the obstructionist, which is how your ex-spouse will portray you, the judge will punish you.

Your ability to present your story depends on:
- ❖ How effective you or your attorney is at explaining your story in writing.
- ❖ How effective you or your attorney is at explaining your story orally.
- ❖ The judge's personal values and biases.
- ❖ The rules of civil procedure and evidence, and how the judge applies them.
- ❖ Your attorney's reputation and relationship with the judge.
- ❖ Your reputation.

Although justice is supposed to be blind, all judges have some biases. They cannot help it. They are people who have lived on this Earth, just as you have. They have been on the bench or practicing family law for many years and, like all of us, they have formed conclusions about the way the world works. No matter how hard a judge tries to be objective, their values and opinions *will* influence their decisions.

Another problem is judicial arrogance. Judges, magistrates, and referees can be patronizing. After years of working in the system, court personnel often believe they have "seen it all." They assume that if you are in the system, it is because you messed up. They think of you as someone who "could not manage their life" and has now come to them to fix it. Many harbor the notion that "you married that person you are now divorcing, you had kids together, and at one time you didn't think they were so bad, so now you must live with the consequences of your choices." What they often fail to understand are the complexities of your situation, especially if your ex-spouse suffers from a mental illness or personality disorder.

Another problem is that your judge's decisions are based only on the information presented to them and what information they are willing to receive. A judge can easily stop reading your brief or stop your attorney mid-sentence, and then rule on your case. Your only recourse is an expensive and time-consuming appeal with little chance of success. Appeals are only successful if the higher court decides that the lower court made an error of law. In family court, where the issues are largely factual and not legal, errors of law are relatively rare.

It is helpful if your attorney knows your judge. If they have been practicing family law for a while, they probably do. Accordingly, your attorney may know the best approach to use with your judge, or what your judge will and will not tolerate. But if your former spouse's attorney has a better relationship with your judge, or is a better storyteller, you may lose regardless of your truths.

Finally, if your personality-disordered former spouse successfully portrays you as "the bad guy," you may never recover your reputation. First impressions stick, court personnel gossip, and you have limited opportunities to interact with your judge. Zoe's former husband refused to take their children to their extracurricular activities during his parenting time. She secured a court order requiring him to do so. In exchange she agreed to do what she had been doing. That is, provide him with the children's schedule. Years later this came back to bite her. Her former husband hired a new attorney to seek more parenting time. Unfamiliar with their case, this attorney accepted the man's spin and presented the old order to the court as evidence of how uncooperative Zoe was. His attorney accepted his version of the truth without question. The attorney was hired to advocate for him, not challenge him. So, she argued that the order requiring Zoe to communicate with the father was entered because Zoe chronically refused to do so. She used that order as evidence to support her client's claim that Zoe was alienating the children from their father. The attorney's job is to represent her client's interests. The next time Zoe was in court, a magistrate who was *not* assigned to her case looked at her and said, "I know all about you." Her ex-husband had damaged her reputation and Zoe was inadvertently complicit.

Every interaction with your judge, then, is an opportunity to look good or be made to look bad.

CREATING YOUR COURTROOM PERSONA

How should Zoe have responded? If she had spent her limited time in front of the judge explaining the "truth" – that the order was designed to correct the father's wrongdoing – several things might have happened:

- ❖ She would have consumed her limited available time; time that might have been spent arguing the current issue – the father's request for more parenting time.
- ❖ She would have allowed her former husband to distract the judge from the real issue.
- ❖ She would have entered a "he-said-she-said" argument that could not be proven without introducing a bevy of historical facts – something the judge will not want to hear.
- ❖ She would have risked damaging her own reputation by appearing defensive and whiny.

Fighting back too hard risks the judge throwing up their hands and saying that *both* parents are in the wrong. Not fighting back at all, risks the judge believing the lies. Zoe was in a *lose-lose* situation. Winning a *lose-lose* scenario is challenging, but it is helpful to cultivate a **Courtroom Persona.** From the very beginning you must "brand" yourself, meticulously managing the "image" you want the judge to see. Once your reputation is established – once the judge forms an opinion – they will be more skeptical of the lies. Your judge is more inclined to trust their own judgment than accept your adversary's accusations.

Like your ex-spouse, you must carefully craft your **Courtroom Persona** both inside and outside the courtroom, because the judge will be exposed to both. In high-conflict cases, the judge is *always* present, even when you are not in court. That is because we all leave paper trails that can be introduced into court as evidence. Emails, telephone records, bank records, even our children's schoolwork may be presented to the judge as evidence supporting your former spouse's "truths." The angry email you wrote after they called you a "bitch" or "bastard" in front of the children will be presented to prove you are not co-parenting and will support your ex-spouse's requests for custody. The email where your ex-spouse called you an "incompetent parent" may be used by both of you: your ex to prove you are incompetent and you to prove they are abusive. Arguing your truth, that you only authored the email after they attacked you for complaining that they were not supervising the children's homework, may only make you look worse to the judge. There is no record of the verbal attacks or actions leading up to the offensive email. But there is that damning email, and how your judge interprets it depends on both of your abilities to spin.

Though your heart may be breaking, the first time you go into the courtroom, and every time thereafter, you must don your persona. Wear it like a costume. This may seem difficult, but it is not. You have been "acting" your entire life. At work or the grocery store, you do not wear your heart on your sleeve. To function, you put aside your feelings and focus on the task at hand. You must do the same whenever you step into the courthouse. Always wear your "professional" costume.

The **Courtroom Persona** that you want to portray is one who is measured and reasonable. The impression you should make is that you *want* your former spouse to have their fair share of parenting time and you *believe* it is important that they have a reasonable amount of time with the children. Most importantly, you want the judge to believe that you are *willing* to resolve these issues. Think of yourself as a diplomat negotiating with a terrorist. The judge represents public opinion. The more reasonable you appear to be, the more unstable your former spouse seems. If you are the calm voice of reason, the judge will gravitate towards your team.

Because final decisions about the division of custody, parenting time and property will not be made until the end of the divorce, your primary task at the first court date is to make a *good first impression.* This does not mean you cannot seek temporary custody of the children or secure whatever financial resources you need. You and your ex-spouse will endure painstaking negotiations – most often outside of the courtroom – to divide your property and establish custody and parenting time. But you *should* propose a temporary parenting plan that sets the groundwork for your claim for full custody. How do you do that? By the power of your **Courtroom Persona.** You must appear *reasonable* and be the *problem-solver*. The message you want to send is "I hear my ex-spouse's concerns, and I am doing my best to address them while still defending my reasons for disagreeing with them" regarding parenting time. You will have to concede and give your former spouse *some* time with the children, so offer something. Do not offer a lot because the court is likely to give them more time than you want them to have. But you do want to appear as if you have been trying to compromise and it is the other parent who is behaving irrationally. But to do so you must rationally speak of *fairness* and *reasonableness*.

The beauty of words like "fair" and "reasonable" is that they are essentially meaningless. That is because they mean different things to different people. A 50-50 split of marital property might seem fair at first glance, but if your former spouse also owns a multi-million-dollar company that you have no access to, it is not. What is fair and reasonable only exists in the eyes of the beholder. They are words that have nothing to do with the reality of your divorce. When you reach a final agreement, which will occur many months after the divorce was initiated, neither of you will feel it is fair or reasonable. No one comes out of a divorce feeling satisfied. These words describe a goal, but not the actual result.

You will have to justify why you believe your proposal is *reasonable*. Communicate concerns about your former spouse in a professional, business-like manner, and *believe* your solution *is* reasonable. Even if you are offering your former spouse only one hour of parenting time a month, believe it is sensible and explain that to the judge. In other words, *whatever* proposal you make is *always reasonable*.

When you speak of custody and parenting time, for example, focus on the *positives*. Speak of what is in your children's *best interests*. These are the magic words because custody and parenting time is decided based on the "best interests of the children" standard. Specifically, what constitutes the "best interest of the child" varies from state to state, but judges generally consider: (1) the parents' and child's wishes for custody arrangements, (2) the relationship of the child with parents, siblings, and others, (3) the child's adjustment to home, school and the community, and (4) the mental and physical health of all people involved. When you argue for custody then (even if it is temporary), the focus of your presentation should be (1) the close bond you and your children share, (2) the close relationship your children have with their grandparents (your parents), their siblings, cousins, etc., (3) the stability of your children's lives with you, and (4) how your children thrive with you and how well you are able to care for them. Speak about how close you and your children are. Give examples.

Do not sling mud. If too much mud is being slung back and forth then the judge becomes irritated with both parents. Judges, like most people, are not really interested in getting involved in your personal wars. They only care about the legal issues. Worse, if you sling more mud than your ex-spouse, the judge might conclude that *you* are the troublesome person, and you will lose ground. Unless your former spouse has a criminal record, you will never convince the judge that your former spouse is evil, and *you will not be validated.*

Focus instead on what you want. It is more difficult for judges to choose between two people arguing for what they want than for the judge to choose between one parent who claims to love their children and the other parent who is badmouthing the first. Do not make it easy on the judge.

For example, imagine you and your former spouse both want to spend Easter Sunday with your children. Your ex argues to the judge that they love their children and want to spend time with them, that the children need them because they have always spent Easter together. You could respond in the following ways: (1) you claim that they are lying, that they did not go to church on the last two Easter Sundays and that after brunch they took a long nap; or (2) you claim that you, too, love your children and that for the past five years you have had special traditions where you take your children to church and you sit and sing together, and then you go out for a special Easter brunch at the children's favorite restaurant. You have already made the reservations and the children are looking forward to continuing this tradition. Which response is more likely to sway the judge to give you what you want? In the first, you have slung mud and the judge might feel obligated to assuage your former spouse's hurt feelings by giving them what they want. After all, here is a parent who wants to spend time with their children. The judge would want to honor that. In the second response, however, you have painted a picture for the judge of your time together with the children and suggested, either overtly or subtly, that it is in the children's best interests that they retain their traditions. Are you guaranteed to win? No, but you are more likely to have the children for church and brunch in the second scenario than you are in the first.

An appropriate courtroom demeanor will also help establish your **Courtroom Persona**. Your demeanor in court should convey that you are respectful and dependable. Demonstrate *respect* by dressing appropriately (business attire), arriving on time, and sitting quietly. Always bring a notepad and pen to court to write notes to your attorney as the other party speaks. These notes will provide your attorney with facts that counter the lies being told about you. You will also appear attentive and restrained when you calmly write corrective notes.

Demonstrate how *dependable* you are by arriving to court early and being prepared. Your preparation includes wearing your **Courtroom Persona**, so take a few additional minutes to psyche yourself up. Never physically react to the judge even if they rule against you. By graciously accepting loss, the judge sees that you are neither impulsive nor reactive, which are personality defects your former spouse is probably trying to apply to you. Nor should you visibly react to your former spouse or their attorney. Do not roll your eyes or shake your head. Instead, stoically write notes to your attorney. If you are in a high-conflict divorce, you will be back in court and will probably re-litigate the same issue. Losing a battle does not mean you will lose the war, but you will reduce your ability to win if you appear as anything other than measured and thoughtful.

BEWARE OF MAGISTRATES AND REFEREES

Not all judges hear all family law matters. Because so many of these motions involve intimate, but legally minor family matters, such as whether Suzie can go on the eighth-grade field trip or who will pay the monthly credit card bill, most judges do not want to hear them. There are too many, and they are relatively trivial. Thus, many court systems have established a triage system. Instead of presenting these issues directly to the judge, the parties argue their case before a designated third party. The third party may be a family law magistrate or a family law counselor. Once that magistrate or counselor renders a decision, the parties may accept it or elect to re-argue their case before the judge.

These third parties are bureaucrats with enormous caseloads. They hear thousands of parents arguing about children's issues and, after a while, most probably seem trivial. Nor do they have time to understand the unique complexities of your case. Sometimes, if they are particularly overburdened, they assume one solution is good for everybody. I heard one family counselor say to a religious father asking for holiday time with his child, "What do holidays matter? You will see your kid the next day or week." Obviously, the father was not too happy to hear that retort and it demonstrates how jaded these court personnel can become. They do not always make the right decision.

Presenting your case to the magistrate or referee involves the same careful planning as presenting your case to the judge. You must appear reasonable and present as if you had tried to resolve the issue but were unsuccessful because of your former spouse.

Always come to court knowing what compromise you will accept and what you will not. Know how far you are willing to bend. This is critical because you do not want to be standing before the decision-maker defending yourself. Why? The request your former spouse is making will *not* appear unreasonable to a third party unfamiliar with your story. Only you, who lives the story, understands why you responded the way you did. Imagine your former spouse is asking to take the kids to visit their mother in Arizona. They want to take the kids on their school break, which is your parenting time this year. You refused the request because the last three times you asked them to accommodate changes in the parenting schedule, they refused.

Why should you now give them what they want? But again, if you try explaining this to the decision-maker, their eyes will glaze over as you carefully recount every time you asked for an accommodation and your ex-spouse refused. They do not care *why* you refused a seemingly reasonable request. Only that you did and now *they* must solve *your* problem.

Instead of recounting the history, focus on the solution. Even though you are before a third-party decision-maker, treat this as if you are negotiating. Begin by offering a solution just shy of what you will not accept. In other words, give in a tiny little bit. Tell the magistrate that you tried resolving the issue with your ex-spouse, but they refused to cooperate. At that moment, your ex-spouse must either address the proposed agreement – at which point the three of you are focused on problem solving and you appear to be the reasonable party – or they will argue that you are lying and uncooperative. If they choose to attack you, allow them a minute to sputter, and then look meaningfully at the magistrate as if to say, "See, this is why we can't agree!" and then proceed to outline your solution. The key is to focus the third party's attention on the issue and not on the mud-slinging. The message you are relaying is, "Yes, this has been a problem in the past, but I have a solution." In that way you acknowledge there have been issues without distracting everyone with the specifics. And you subliminally convince the decision maker that the *real* issue here is your ex-spouse's unreasonableness, not yours.

Before going to court, try to realistically assess your chances of winning. If you are likely to lose, keep in mind several things. First, you are at risk of losing a battle, not the war. Maintain your perspective. Second, again, consider what you want in exchange for gracefully "giving in." Anything you get in exchange for finally agreeing to allow your ex-spouse to take the children to Arizona is a "win" you did not have before. And third, while there is no "bank account" with your ex-spouse (they will not remember that you ultimately agreed to their demand – only that they went to court and "won"), you may build a cache of good-will with the magistrate or counselor. That too is a win.

Consider proposing a comprehensive solution that extends beyond the presenting issue. If deviations from the parenting plan have been an ongoing problem for you and your ex-spouse, arrive at court with a proposal for how you and your former spouse will manage proposed changes in the parenting schedule going forward. This is your own way of "upping the ante." Perhaps each party is obligated to agree to the proposed change unless there is a compelling reason not to. Perhaps there will be no changes allowed – ever. Perhaps the two of you must see a mediator or parent-coordinator to resolve proposed change requests. Whatever you propose, there are two advantages to this comprehensive approach. First, you may blindside your ex-spouse, deflecting the conversation away from this singular issue to a more global issue of modifying the parenting plan, forcing them to catch up. The magistrate or referee will not wait too long for their response and the pressure may muddle their thinking. They may agree to a term that, had they more time, they would not ordinarily have agreed to.

Second, by making it more difficult for both of you to change the parenting time schedule, your ex-spouse may begin to understand that if they want something they will have to jump through hoops. They cannot approach you directly, as they had in the past, and browbeat you into submission. By taking control away from both parties, your abusing former spouse now must play by the rules. Either they will do so, or they will avoid you completely, never again asking for a deviation. Either way, you have eliminated the frustration of ending up in court because they want something you are unwilling to give.

SEE AND BE SEEN

It is essential that you be out in the community with your kids. This is especially true if you are in a more traditional marriage where you are the father who has left much of the child rearing to your wife. Go to your daughter's dance recital games. Go to school conferences. Walk your young child into class and say hello to the teacher. Get to know the other parents, coaches, and teachers. Start making your child's lunch and start doing the grocery shopping. Buy your children their school clothes and that book they need for English class. Volunteer. And *keep track of everything you do.*

There are several reasons for getting involved now. The big one is that if you are going to ask for custody, or joint physical custody, you must be able to show the court you are an involved parent. Your claims will go a long way if you can stand in court and say, "Jeremy hates peanut butter, so I make tuna for lunch," or something to that effect. If your children's teachers and coaches can provide affidavits on your behalf that offer the court independent verification of your claims, this will enhance your *reliability.* But these folks will only help if they know you. Zoe's former husband was not at all involved in his child's life. But once the divorce started, he made sure to charm the preschool teacher and she wrote a lovely affidavit about what a concerned parent he was, and how he prepared nutritious lunches for his son. According to the mother, it was not at all true. Her best response, rather than getting into the "he-said-she-said" dilemma, was to fight back with her own set of affidavits affirming her own parenting involvement.

Second, once you do have your children alone with you, whether you have full or partial custody, you will need to be parenting. You *must not rely* on your former spouse to parent for you. You cannot, for example, rely on your former spouse to tell you when conferences and talent shows are scheduled. That was the old dynamic and, if you continue to engage, it will be much more difficult to extricate yourself from their abuse and you will actually increase your post-divorce conflict. This is because the more engaged you remain with your former spouse; the more opportunities exist for them to continue old behavior patterns. Better to start developing your independent parenting skills sooner rather than later. Not only will it help you in court, but it will help develop your relationship with your children as a single parent as well.

Not everyone in your community will believe you are righteous, and your ex-spouse is evil. Some people will not want to get involved. Some people will take sides. Some people will simply walk away. It is not worth your time trying to win those people back into your life. You cannot anticipate how each friend, acquaintance, or professional will interpret a situation they know little about. How people interpret a situation says more about them than about you. Sarah attended a meeting at her son's school. Her former husband, who had not been an involved parent but was now trying to gain full custody, approached her while she chatted with another mother. The two women were not close friends. At that moment, Sarah's ex-husband reached into his wallet and handed her a check to repay her some money he owed. After he walked away, the other mother observed that he could have paid Sarah in private but obviously did it in public so he would appear responsible. She saw through Sarah's ex-husband.

On the other hand, Zoe's former husband successfully "won over" their son's preschool teacher. Zoe had prided herself on her cooking skills. Every night she prepared gourmet dinners for her family. Her ex-husband never went into the kitchen. Their toddler, raised on fresh vegetables and salmon, happened to develop a taste for Chef Boyardee Ravioli. It was a completely processed and unhealthy food but Zoe, as a treat during the divorce, occasionally gave it to her son for lunch. Her ex-husband prepared peanut butter sandwiches for the child on his parenting time, even though the boy did not really like peanut butter. For the **temporary orders** hearing, the teacher prepared an affidavit in favor of the father, noting that he prepared wholesome and nutritious meals for the child's lunch. Zoe was furious. The teacher did not understand the dynamics of what she had witnessed. There was no point, however, in Zoe wasting her time trying to win over this teacher by explaining the facts to her. Once the school year ended, the child never returned to that school. Zoe never saw the teacher again.

How people interpret what they observe depends on their own experience and wisdom. Knowing that, spend your energies fighting the important battles rather than trying to preserve your good name to strangers. The only way you can win the public relations game is to be yourself and do what you believe is right. Do not waste time on people whose opinions ultimately do not matter.

CHAPTER THREE:

Many people rely on their lawyers to help them manage their divorce. While some people successfully manage their own divorces, especially those whose divorces are amicable, the system is not designed to help unrepresented litigants. Lawyers and judges speak about "access to justice," but the reality is that non-lawyers are required to adhere to the same standards as lawyers. They are charged with understanding and abiding by the complex rules of civil procedure and are punished for making mistakes. Access to justice is largely a myth.

If you cannot afford an attorney, educate yourself. You can learn much about the legal process from the Internet. Many divorce attorneys post basic information on their websites. Your state bar association has information for "pro se" litigants – people who come to court unrepresented. And there are articles written by attorneys and judges posted as well. There are plenty of books about divorce to peruse. Finally, take advantage of Legal Aid clinics in your community as well.

Even if an attorney will represent you, educate yourself as much as possible before you make an appointment, so you do not waste your time asking about the basics. Ask instead about the issues that still confuse you.

As you study, focus on two things: the basics of family law and the rules of civil procedure. The laws of divorce can be bundled into three categories: custody and parenting time, division of property and debt, allocation of income. Statutes, the laws created by your state's legislature, can be vague. Many states do not define what constitutes the "best interests of the child," for example. Some states, like Michigan, do. But even those definitions can be vague. One of the "best interest" factors in Michigan is the "reasonable preference of the child." Determining what is reasonable depends on the facts and circumstances of individual cases. Lawyers review past cases to refine the meaning of vague terms. Locating those cases is challenging. Some Internet sites, such as *Google Scholar* and *FindLaw,* publish them. Remember to look only at the statutes and cases from your state. Laws from other states have no authority in yours.

The Rules of Civil Procedure are extremely important. They are the guidelines for maneuvering through the court system. Most states publish their rules on the Internet. They may also provide forms for you to download and use. The rules are confusing, but you do not need to learn all of them. Focus on the most critical. First are the rules of Service of Process. Whenever you start a legal action against your former spouse, you must give a copy of the paperwork to your former spouse. You must also *prove* to the court that you did so. This rule is founded in our Constitution, so it is especially important. If you do not prove to the judge that you **served** (delivered) a copy of your paperwork to your spouse, the judge does not have authority to hear your case and it will be thrown out of their courtroom. You will have wasted your time and money.

The reverse also holds true. If your former spouse fails to serve you or provide proof of service to the court, let the judge know. It does not matter that you are standing in the courtroom telling the judge that you were not notified of the legal action. The judge has no **jurisdiction** or authority to decide their case. Once in court I observed a young woman who was trying to increase her child support. She had **served** her **motion** (request) on her baby's father but did not file a **proof of service** with the court. She did not verify that she had served him. Still, he was present, as was his attorney who argued that her motion should be dismissed because she failed to file her **proof of service.** The judge agreed. At first, this seems ridiculous since the father was obviously served and knew about the hearing, but the judge was correct. If she had ruled on the issue, perhaps ordering the father to pay more child support, he might have appealed. Her decision would be overturned by the court of appeals because the mother had plainly violated the rules. In the end, she would have spent time and money without achieving any result. Serving your opponent is essential and so is letting the court know that you did.

The second critical issue is timing. All courts have rules about when you can schedule the **hearing** (presentation to the judge). After you file a legal action, your former spouse may respond in writing. You can then reply to their response. Remember that your reply must be filed with the court – so the judge can read your statement – and served on your former spouse. The rules of civil procedure allow time for these documents to be exchanged.

Finally, whenever you go to court – whether you are the person filing the legal action or responding to it – you should know exactly what you are asking the court to do. If your state allows, you should bring to court a **proposed order** which outlines your desired outcome. If the judge rules in your favor, ask if you can present it to them. Always bring a copy for your former spouse. The judge may amend your **order** or prepare their own. Whatever document they sign, make certain it is filed with the clerk and that you keep a copy for your records. You will need to refer to that **order** when conflicts with your former spouse arise.

CHOOSING YOUR ATTORNEY

Law is a business and lawyers are in it to make money. Choosing the right attorney for you also means looking beyond the marketing. When researching attorneys, you will encounter websites with various visual motifs. Some have charming pictures of parents and children walking together on a beach. Others display tailored attorneys aggressively postured before a judge. Remember this is all imagery. Like everyone else, attorneys work to earn a living. Do not accept the marketing as testament to who that person really is. Do not be fooled by advertisements that express compassion for what you are going through. Not all attorneys are sympathetic. Nor should you be taken in by the attorney who vows to "fight for your rights." Many attorneys are in the business *just* to make money. And finally, while you want an experienced family law attorney, you do not want someone who runs a divorce factory and treats your case in cookie-cutter fashion. One size does not fit all.

You must scrutinize prospective attorneys to determine whether you can work well together. You do not want someone who will dictate to you and expect you to follow blindly. Nor do you want someone who leaves every decision to you. You want a partner, but a partner who is experienced in the laws of divorce. You and your attorney should collaborate. You should be able to discuss strategies with them and participate in negotiations. While they know the law, you know your story. You can anticipate the repercussions of prospective legal actions and discuss them. This helps you avoid surprises and prepare for different outcomes. An experienced attorney can also give you invaluable advice. If they tell you to stop talking to your ex-spouse about the issues and let them manage the negotiations, do as they say. You do not want to risk undermining the strategy you and your attorney have developed.

It can be difficult finding the attorney that is right for you. The best way to find an attorney is through referrals and then by interviewing prospective lawyers. When you ask friends and family to refer you to a "good" attorney," however, remember that your situation might be different than the person making the referral. Their divorce goals might not be the same as yours. Their former spouse might not present the same complications as yours. So, ask why your friend recommends that attorney and how that attorney resolved particularly difficult issues. Focus on the process the attorney used, not just the result.

Some attorneys charge for the initial consultations, others do not. If you cannot afford to interview multiple attorneys, and the person you are primarily interested in charges, then meet first with attorneys who do not charge. Use those meetings to practice seeing past the marketing to the real attorney. Remember that attorneys who appear in court are particularly good at posturing and performing. Their primary job is to persuade you to believe in them. They will use those skills to secure new clients. It is important, then, to do your research before selecting your attorney. Mistakes can be time consuming and costly.

BE PREPARED

Even if you hire an attorney, you must educate yourself about the law. Once you understand the fundamental legal issues, you and your attorney can spend your time together focusing on strategy. You already know that the primary issues in divorce are custody and parenting time, property and debt division, and allocation of income. Focus conversations with your attorney on *why* you deserve custody and *why* your former spouse does not. Be specific. To the best of your ability, focus on verifiable facts, not emotions. If you feel comfortable, outline for your attorney the parenting plan you would like implemented and use that as a starting point. If you are at first unsure how to achieve your goals, do not worry. Everything will be worked out later. Regarding property and debt division, if you again believe you are entitled to more than fifty percent of the property and less than fifty percent of the debt, explain to your attorney precisely why. Again, be specific. Also explain why you deserve spousal support if that is what you are seeking.

Let your attorney know how temperamental your ex-spouse is. I always asked my clients how their former spouse managed their anger because that helped me understand what I was up against.

Lastly, when you ask your attorney intelligent questions, you are not only saving time and money, but you are informing them that you are an educated consumer. This will engender respect and smooth the path towards collaboration. By identifying your reasons, you help your attorney develop the theme of your case and establish its trajectory. Strategy matters and your case will be less *reactive* and more *proactive*, enabling you to maintain some control over a process that feels, and often is, entirely out of your hands.

When you meet with your attorney, bring copies of important documents. Label them or select another way to organize them so you do not waste time and money sorting through paperwork. Important papers include:

- ❖ Tax returns from the last three years.
- ❖ Both you and your former spouse's Federal W-2 forms from the last three years.
- ❖ The deed to your house and any other real property you own.
- ❖ Title to your cars and any other motor vehicles you own.
- ❖ Statements from all your savings, checking, and investment accounts from the last three years.
- ❖ Statements from you and your former spouse's retirement accounts from the last three years.
- ❖ Your most recent credit card bills.
- ❖ Any other documents you believe are important, such as income tax returns from a business you or your former spouse own, or statements evidencing debt you owe others or that others owe you.

Never give your attorney your only copies of these documents. Should the two of you have an irreconcilable disagreement, you will waste time trying to recover them.

YOUR RELATIONSHIP
WITH YOUR ATTORNEY IS LIMITED

Your attorney is not your friend. They have been trained in the laws of divorce and their only job is to present your story to the judge and persuade them to decide in your favor. Never forget that attorneys charge by the hour, so the longer you take to share your story, the more money it will cost you. Your attorney will not reduce your bill because you need a shoulder to cry on. Also, because your state is a **no-fault** state, which means neither party needs to claim the other was at fault for causing the divorce, the emotional abuse you have suffered is not legally relevant. It simply does not matter, so do not waste money sharing those stories with your attorney.

Your attorney is not your therapist. They are not trained to discuss your feelings but will still charge you for their time. Your attorney views your situation through only one lens: the legal lens. You are paying them to help you deconstruct your current life, but they cannot assist you in reconstructing it. While you are divorcing, you will also need to plan your future and your attorney is not the resource to help you. They are neither your career counselor nor financial adviser. There are plenty of professionals out there to consult with; and if you do not want to spend money on them, then invest in a few books or bounce ideas off close friends and family. Your attorney is only *one tool in your toolbox*. Do not rely on them for everything.

Recognize that your attorney's effectiveness is limited by how you present your story. You are experiencing an enormous life transition, and this creates inner turmoil and inner conflict. One day you may want to go to trial, the next day you may not. You are likely to convey these conflicting emotions to your attorney. Therefore, you must be mindful of the messages you give. Allen was extremely concerned about the cost of a trial, so his attorney encouraged him to settle. In doing so, he lost an opportunity to "leverage" more from his former wife by threatening her with an expensive trial. Dan was lonely and interested in dating, so his attorney encouraged him to relinquish physical custody of the children. Neither of these situations worked out ideally and both resulted in costly post-judgment litigation. When you meet with your attorney, prepare yourself by knowing your objectives and be sure to send the message that is correct for you.

It is important to visit a therapist if you are struggling with your emotions. Visit a career counselor if you are uncertain about your employment prospects. Visit a financial adviser or educate yourself by attending seminars or reading books. Do not use your attorney for anything other than legal advice. Your attorney's job is to help you preserve your legal rights and represent you in court. The strategies the two of you develop are only part of the big picture – the legal part. Your divorce involves more than just maneuvering through the courtroom. Your divorce involves restructuring your entire life. Recognize that your attorney is only *part* of your team. You must assume the role of head coach.

ELIMINATING YOUR EX-SPOUSE'S OPTIONS

Even if you are uncertain that divorce is imminent, it is wise to select an attorney while you are thinking clearly, rather than in the heat of the moment when you are served with divorce papers and your emotions are surging. Interviewing and selecting an attorney early can be beneficial. It can also eliminate the competition.

Attorneys are required by their ethics to protect client confidences. If you speak to an attorney about your case, they cannot share that information with others. Nor can they represent someone who may oppose you in court. That creates a conflict of interest for the attorney, something also prohibited by the rules of professional conduct. If you are concerned your spouse will hire an aggressive attorney, one with a reputation for being especially unreasonable, then you may want to interview that attorney first. By sharing your confidences, you create a **conflict of interest** between that attorney and your spouse, and that attorney is prohibited by the **ethical canons** from representing your spouse.

It will likely cost you a couple of hundred dollars to "**conflict out**" these aggressive attorneys, but it may also save you money overall. Meet with the top ten tough attorneys in your area, and you have limited your spouse's choices of who represents them against you, especially among those who might drive up your costs by refusing to cooperate or aggressively filing motions in court.

FIRING YOUR ATTORNEY

Your attorney is your advocate, hired to represent you. Still, it is a business relationship that can sour. To minimize misunderstandings, keep copies of all correspondence between you and your lawyer. If you exchange emails, do not delete them. File them. You should also keep copies of every substantive letter your attorney sends to your former spouse's attorney (cover letters need not be saved) and final copies of all legal **pleadings** (documents filed in court). If you and your attorney are working together, you will have several drafts of pleadings before you approve the final document. You do not need to preserve the drafts unless they contain information that the two of you agreed to exclude but might prove relevant later. In that case, highlight the vital information and file it for future use. But you should always have copies of final documents your attorney files with the court and substantive letters between them and your ex-spouse's attorney. Finally, it is imperative that you keep copies of all judicial orders in your case.

To avoid misunderstandings, send follow-up emails to your attorney after meeting, talking on the phone, or exchanging emails. Send an email summarizing what you two agreed would be the next step in your case. High-conflict divorces generate substantial amounts of litigation, and this will help you monitor your case's progress. A record of what is supposed to occur will also help you identify if something did not happen that was supposed to. Use a large calendar to help you keep track of dates. For example, if your attorney plans to send a discovery request to your ex-spouse, the calendar will remind you to call 28 days later to learn whether they answered. You will also know if your attorney did what they had promised to do. You do not want months to pass before realizing your attorney has done nothing to advance your case. The calendar will help you identify discrepancies should you decide to petition the court for a change of attorney. Recognize that even after you have hired your attorney, you may still not get the results you want. Sometimes what you want is simply not possible. It is rare, for example, for one parent to get complete custody over the child, no matter how awful you think that other parent is. Sometimes the other attorney might simply be better than yours. Perhaps your attorney is inexperienced or burnt-out, too busy, or has a bad reputation with the judge. It may be necessary to replace your attorney. Before doing so, determine whether your expectations are reasonable. Consult with friends and family. Talk to your attorney and listen with a critical ear. If you elect to replace them, know that this will cause a delay in your case, but better that your case takes longer than have to spend time and money correcting mistakes later.

PREPARING TO FILE

Most people engage in much soul-searching before filing for divorce. When you marry, you expect to spend the rest of your life with your chosen partner. Realizing you have made a mistake, or the relationship has deteriorated in ways you never could have imagined, is painful. Your marriage was a commitment to certain expectations. Your divorce is an acknowledgment that those expectations will never come to fruition.

When a marriage is ending, different scenarios play out. Perhaps you had been considering filing for divorce but was afraid. Even a difficult situation can be more comfortable than the unknown because it is familiar. Perhaps your spouse has been threatening a divorce and you are terrified of the consequences, knowing you will lose so much. Or perhaps your spouse has demanded a divorce and left no opportunity for reconsideration. In that case, there is little you can do. However, if you find yourself in the untenable situation of facing an irreparably damaged marriage but are afraid of making a change, remember that doing nothing empowers your spouse to continue their abuse. They will continue the status quo until something gives. Eventually you must step up to the plate. That does not necessarily mean filing for divorce, but it does mean preparing yourself. Whether you are contemplating filing for divorce, you are concerned your spouse might file, or you have that knot in your stomach telling you things are not as they should be, you need to take control over the documents of your life. This means copying and securing important documents.

When you are married, you are legally entitled to unmitigated access to your financial documents. Some people do not know that, however. This may be because you and your spouse divided responsibilities and your spouse's documents are located in their office or desk. Or it may be because your spouse's documents are password protected. To conclude the divorce, all the information will eventually be revealed; however, it is far less expensive and time-consuming to gather the information before the divorce is filed, rather than after when the only way to retrieve them is through formal **discovery**. Better to keep a set of documents for yourself than to rely on your attorney and the court system to get them for you. Even if you and your spouse remain married, it is always good to understand your finances.

The documents you need fall into three categories: assets, debt, and income.

ASSETS

Your assets include real and personal property. Real property consists of land and things attached or affixed to the land. Personal property consists of everything else. For most people, the family home is the most valuable asset. Next are retirement and investment accounts, cars, and toys (such as boats and recreational vehicles) and finally jewelry, art, and furniture. Copy and preserve these important documents:

❖ Deed to the house.

❖ Deed to other real property, such as a vacation home or time-share.

❖ Most recent appraisals – if available – of all real property.

❖ Most recent statements from all checking accounts.

❖ Most recent statements from all savings accounts.

❖ Most recent statements from all investment accounts.

❖ Most recent statements from all retirement accounts.

❖ Titles to the cars.

❖ Titles to other motor vehicles, such as boats, jet skis, and snowmobiles.

❖ Appraisals for valuables, such as art and jewelry.

❖ Life insurance policies.

❖ Statements of money or property owed to you or your spouse (e.g., promissory notes).

When taking stock of your assets, consider things that might not seem obvious at first. Do you have a membership to a country club or swim club? Do you or your spouse have stock options from work? What about frequent flyer miles? All of these are assets that will be divided should you divorce. And if you do not divorce, taking stock of your wealth is always a feel-good exercise.

Finally, walk through your house and videotape all your property. Include furniture, fine china and silver, art, and jewelry. Also take photographs or videos of everything of sentimental value to you. This way, if something disappears or is destroyed, you have proof that the property existed and its apparent value. You are also in a better position to deny your former spouse if they claim that *you* destroyed the property, as you had already gone to the trouble of videotaping to preserve it.

PROTECTING YOUR ASSETS

Protecting liquid assets – money – should be a primary concern. Before the complaint for divorce is filed, you have equal right to all marital assets. If you are concerned that your spouse may drain your accounts once they discover you have filed for divorce, you may take fifty percent of your marital assets. You do not need to hide this money. In fact, you should not. Instead, the money should be preserved in a separate bank account. Acknowledge to the court that you are protecting your share of the marital assets before it is wasted by your angry spouse. Timing is important. If you know your spouse will become enraged by your actions, move the money only moments before you file for divorce. Then suggest to your spouse that they file a motion in court to resolve the issue.

Dan was attached to his car. It was the family's third vehicle and his personal "toy." Worried that his wife would damage it in anger, he moved it into a storage facility. By fully disclosing his actions he was not hiding assets, the asset would be considered in the division of property, but it would also be safe. Meredith hid her jewelry. She gave it to her mother to protect. In that situation, however, her husband completely forgot about the valuable diamonds and the property was never valued when the assets were divided.

Some people feel inclined to waste some money to ease their pain. Before the complaint for divorce is filed, half of the marital property is theirs, so it is theirs to waste. Meredith bought herself a lot of jewelry before she filed for divorce. Her reasoning was that her husband would not want it and so it was an asset she was sure to keep. Allen wanted to join friends on a trip to Las Vegas, so he borrowed against his 401K. He would be required to pay the penalty for early withdrawal, but he was willing to do that. The debt became a marital debt, and, in the settlement, Allen agreed to assume the entire retirement debt in exchange for his ex-wife taking on an equivalent amount of credit card debt. Allen reasoned he would rather pay himself back than a credit card company. While Allen's ex-wife paid strangers, he paid himself. For Allen, it was a win-win. In both cases, Meredith and Allen shifted assets. Allen still paid for his vacation and Meredith retained her jewels in place of other assets, but each made choices they were willing to live with.

DEBT

Regarding debt, the general rule is that the person receiving the asset, receives the debt that corresponds with it. Thus, if you are awarded the marital home, you will also be solely responsible for the mortgage. If you are awarded your car, you will be solely responsible for your car loan as well. When collecting documents evidencing debt, copy:

- ❖ Mortgage documents, including most recent statements.
- ❖ Automobile loan documents, including most recent statements.
- ❖ Loan documents for other vehicles, including most recent statements.
- ❖ Most recent credit card statements.
- ❖ Statements of money or property you or your spouse owe to others.

Like assets, there may be "hidden" debt such as the membership to the swim club. Be certain to include those. Your net worth is the difference between your assets and debt. Estimate that in the event of divorce, you will receive approximately half of that net worth, less what you and your spouse pay for attorney's fees.

INCOME

To calculate income, copy the following documents:

❖ Federal and state income tax returns for the last three to five years.

❖ W-2 forms.

❖ Statements from any source that provides regular income to you or your spouse.

If you or your spouse receive regular income from a trust or annuity, that should also be considered part of your gross income.

The more difficult situation is if your spouse owns their own business, and you know that not all the income has been reported. If your spouse is hiding income from the Internal Revenue Service, it is likely they will hide income from you. In this difficult situation, you must record the things money is spent on. You must prove to the court that your lifestyle is not supported by your reported income. You can do this by showing receipts for the expensive items you and your spouse purchased, or the trips the two of you took together. Take photos of the new boat, preferably with your spouse standing at the bow. Preserve the airline tickets from that vacation and photograph your spouse wearing any new and expensive clothing, watches, or jewelry. Compare those to the absence of credit card debt and the miniscule, reported income that could not possibly have supported your lifestyle, and hopefully you will convince the judge that your spouse's actual income is higher than they claim.

WHERE TO KEEP THE DOCUMENTS YOU COPY

Once you have copies of these documents and photos, secure them in a safe place, such as at your work or with a trusted family member or friend. If divorce is not imminent, then a copy of your most recent income tax return – along with 1099s, W-2s, and other year-end statements – will probably suffice. If you believe divorce may happen sooner rather than later, then copy at least three years of statements. Do not hide the originals, as you will be required to produce them.

CHAPTER FOUR:

A divorce begins with the filing of a **complaint** or **petition**. Complaints are stories. They tell the court who the parties are, what the issue is, and what the plaintiff or petitioner wants. Because all states are **no-fault**, fault does not need to be alleged. The plaintiff simply states that the marriage is no longer viable and that they want a divorce. Some states dictate this language. In Michigan, for example, the law requires the plaintiff to allege that "there has been a breakdown of the marriage relationship to the extent that the objects of matrimony have been destroyed and there remains no reasonable likelihood that the marriage can be preserved." In Washington State, all the plaintiff needs to say is that the "marriage is irretrievably broken."

It is essential the plaintiff reveal where the parties live to establish that the court has **jurisdiction**. Jurisdiction is the court's authority to prevail over your case. Because the laws of matrimony are derived from the state, only a state court has jurisdiction over your marriage and divorce. A Minnesota court, for example, can only grant a divorce to a couple living in Minnesota. The Minnesota court may not grant a divorce to a couple living in Massachusetts.

For a state to acquire jurisdiction over a divorcing couple, the plaintiff must have lived in that state for a minimum amount of time.

The time differs, but if you have concerns about the demise of your marriage, consider that your spouse may have an ulterior motive for asking you to move. I know one father who convinced his wife to relocate back to the state where he had grown up. She agreed, leaving behind family and friends. Six months after they moved, when the minimum jurisdiction requirement in the new state had been met, he filed for divorce. He had planned ahead.

Jurisdiction is also important to establish that the court has the exclusive right to make custody determinations over your children. Many courts require the plaintiff to allege that their state is also the children's home state, that the children and at least one parent have significant connections to that state, that no other state claims jurisdiction over the children, and that no other custody action is pending in another state. The requirement that these assertions be made arises from laws generated to reduce the risk of parental kidnapping or forum shopping, where parents move from state to state seeking a more favorable custody determination.

If your former spouse lives in a state different from you and the children, beware of them filing for custody there. One way they might do this is by asking that the children visit, then keeping them for six months. Six months is the amount of time the statute delineates for establishing a child's home state. If you suspect this is your former spouse's plan, retrieve the children before the six months expire. Do not agree, in writing, that they may keep the children for that amount of time. Do not agree to modify the parenting plan. Do send a copy of your parenting plan or judgment of divorce to the sheriff's office in the county where your former spouse resides and ask for assistance retrieving your children.

If you are still married and your spouse lives in a different state, and then keeps the children in that state for an extended amount of time, you are free to retrieve them. Your spouse cannot claim you kidnapped the children because you have legal rights. If you do *not* bring your children home, however, you risk your spouse success-fully arguing that "substantial evidence" is available in *their* state concerning the children's "care, protection, training and personal re-lationships." In other words, they will have documentation and wit-nesses to prove that the children really live with them in *their* "home state."

Retrieving the children from a different state may be difficult and the police may not help because your spouse did not kidnap them. Like you, they have legal rights. Only when the divorce is filed and the court assumes jurisdiction, will you be able to ask for help. Once the court has power over your case, the judge can issue temporary custody arrangements and if your ex-spouse defies them, they would be defying the judge's order. Judges do not like that. But without a custody order, perhaps because you and your child's other parent never married, you may have more legal rights than the other parent. I know of one woman who took her child to visit her baby's father in another state. He refused to return the child. When she asked the po-lice for help, they refused because she had told them the baby's father was holding the child. She returned home devastated until I advised her to let the police know there was no custody order and the baby's father had no legal rights to the child. Upon learning that, the police were able to intervene and recover the child.

The remainder of the complaint contains general allegations about the primary issues in your case: the plaintiff alleges that they deserve custody, that the other party should get reasonable parenting time, and that there is property and debt to be divided. If the plaintiff wants spousal support, they must also allege that they have a need. You do not need to be specific. For example, you do not need to state that your home is worth $100,000 or that you and your spouse have $22,000 of credit card debt. Nor do you need to outline the terms of the "reasonable" parenting plan you propose. The specifics of the divorce will be decided later.

You will need to ask the court to give you what you want. In the last section of the **complaint**, called the **prayer for relief**, you will ask the judge:

- ❖ To grant you a divorce.
- ❖ To give you custody of the minor children.
- ❖ To give the other parent reasonable parenting time.
- ❖ To divide assets and debt.

If you are seeking alimony, also known as **spousal support**, you would ask for it here.

Be prepared for your spouse to react angrily to your request for custody. Even if you had agreed – which you would not have done if you are facing a high-conflict divorce – it is painful for any parent to face the loss of custody of their children. For some parents, especially personality-disordered parents, your request for custody is seen as a declaration of war. Should you receive a violent reaction, soothe your angry spouse by blaming your attorney. Tell them that this is what you were advised to do, and it will all be worked out later. That does not mean you will relinquish your claim for custody. It is merely a way to reduce the tension. Do *not*, however, agree to anything in writing. If you are pressed, hide behind your attorney, and explain to your spouse that your attorney said this is the way the law is, and it will all be worked out in the end.

TO FILE OR NOT TO FILE

If you are married to an emotionally abusive spouse, you have probably been thinking about divorce for years. But change is exceedingly difficult. You may feel inadequate, having lost confidence in your ability to make it alone in the world. This is a result of your circumstances. For years you have been told you cannot do anything right. Every decision you make is wrong and hurtful, and you find yourself repeatedly apologizing to make things right. You chase after a fleeting horizon of "correct responses" you can never reach. You never know which choice will result in your spouse's approval or disapproval. And your apologies to keep the peace are never enough because at any moment you might unintentionally mess up and incur your spouse's wrath once again.

What are your fears? Everything. You have given your spouse all the power. Even if you are the breadwinner, you fear losing half or more of the assets. You fear their claim that you will lose your children. You fear losing your home and your place in the community. You fear being alone. And you fear the shame of validating their final insult – that you really are a loser who could not even keep your family together.

I have known many people trapped in this situation. As much as they hate it, they are comfortable. They live with the paradigm that the enemy they know is better than the enemy they do not know. They tell themselves they are providing a stable home for their children, and perhaps they will make a change later, when the children are grown or when they retire. I have encouraged these souls to consider that while they are preserving the status quo, they are also enabling and validating their spouse's behavior. They are teaching their children that it is okay to remain in an emotionally abusive relationship. They are teaching their children to accept disrespect. Or they are teaching their children to emulate the abusive behavior. Studies often conclude that exposure to violence in the home is a significant factor in predicting a child's violent behavior. Witnessing violence between one's parent or caretaker is the strongest risk factor of transmitting violent behavior from one generation to the next.

If, on the other hand, you establish your own household where everyone is treated with dignity and respect, you teach your children that an alternative lifestyle exists. You demonstrate there is more than one way to interact in a relationship. Furthermore, this new lifestyle will likely appeal to your children, who probably long for respect and acceptance, too. If you are living in a household where you are constantly walking on eggshells, then your children are probably walking on those very same eggshells, too. Studies have found that thirty to sixty percent of perpetrators of intimate partner violence also abuse children in the household. How liberating for all of you to be free of that emotional burden.

There is no doubt divorce is costly. When contemplating filing for divorce you must weigh the financial cost of leaving with the emotional cost of staying. Add to that equation that it may take as much as ten years to recover financially. But your emotional recovery will occur far sooner.

If you decide to file for divorce, be aware that you are entering a dangerous phase of your 'relationship.' Studies have shown that physical violence escalates when one spouse tries to leave. Have a plan. Consult with the local shelter. Keep a bag of clothes for you and your children in the back of your car. Stockpile some cash. Know where you will go if you need to escape.

If you decide to file for divorce, you must also prepare yourself emotionally. Think about how your spouse will respond and then prepare your response. If your spouse is likely to be violent, then have your escape plan ready. If your spouse is likely to scream and yell, decide how you will respond. Will you scream back? Will you respond with silence? Will you agree to talk if they calm down? Will you agree to withdraw the papers and go to therapy? Under what circumstances would you be willing to do that?

Once you have filed for divorce, you have changed the dynamics of your relationship. What will you ask for in return for remaining in the marriage? The things you ask for must be specific and concrete. Asking an emotionally abusive person to be more respectful will not accomplish anything. They will have any number of reasons justifying why they behave as they do, and much of the blame will fall on you. Instead, think of the top five things they do that hurt you and provide them with specific alternative behaviors. Give them time to change, knowing they are likely to fail at the beginning, and set a date in the future when the two of you can evaluate their progress and you can contemplate your future. If, as you are reading this you are thinking it will never work, then consider focusing the dialogue with your spouse on the terms of the divorce and not on keeping the marriage together.

Steel yourself against your spouse's threats that they will take everything from you. Remember, the chance of them getting all the property and sole custody of the children is slim. Nor should you agree to anything they offer at this early stage. You have time to think and plan. Use that time. Agree to consider the offer. If the offer is limited or conditional, then it is not worth considering. Do not be afraid you will not get another offer or a better deal. You have legal rights, and you can negotiate for more.

Do not fall into the old trap of thinking you must be "fair." If you are thinking that being fair will appease your spouse and reduce the anger they unleashed on you when they were served with the divorce papers, you are wrong. Have you *ever* been able to smooth things over or are their emotions entirely independent of you? Even if they accepted your apology for buying the wrong brand of milk, will they soon become angry about something else, such as the size of the cereal box? If the answer is yes, then do not give up your rights at the starting gate, on the off chance that things will be different now. You must start off strong. Change the paradigm and weaken their power. If they can no longer predict your responses with certainty, then they cannot push your buttons as easily as they have done in the past.

By starting out conciliatory, you are telling your spouse that the same familiar rules apply. By starting out strong, you are changing the game. Now is time to protect yourself and your children. Do not give in because you are sad you have lost your partner. If you and your spouse were truly partners, even if you were getting divorced, this scenario would be entirely different. You and your spouse truly would be working together for the best interests of your children. But now you are in a *chess game,* and you need to think *three moves ahead.*

Some couples decide to divorce and reach agreement on all-important issues. Together they chose who will file for divorce. Those are not the high-conflict cases unless one person bullied the other into agreeing to their terms. If you feel forced to accept terms that your gut says are not right, trust your inner voice. Do not sign. Take the papers to a lawyer of your choosing for review. Do not go to the attorney your spouse recommends even if they claim it will save money. You have a right to independent counsel, and it is an ethical violation for lawyers to represent both parties in a divorce. And you will spend more money undoing what you agreed to than the money you will spend getting it right the first time.

It may be difficult not to sign, especially if your ex-spouse relentlessly bullies you. Hold out as long as you can, but if you must give in and sign, do so in a way that enables you to renege. You must not sign your legal name. If you properly sign and date the legal documents, you will not have any credibility claiming later that you were forced to sign. It will be their word against yours and they will have your proper signature as proof. Instead, try spelling your name wrong and then cross it out with fat strokes. Make the strokes so fat you will be forced to re-sign over the legal terminology. Another option is to sign using the wrong middle name. Use your mother's name or even your ex-spouse's. In either case, the purpose is to provide doubt that *you* signed the documents. When your former spouse complains, explain that you were so upset you did not know what you were doing. But inside, you know that without your proper legal signature the judge will not approve that divorce.

If you and your spouse are contemplating divorce and you both agree that your spouse will file, do not be surprised if they breach any agreement you reached and asks for "more." If you had agreed to joint custody and the complaint asks for full custody, it is probably because their attorney convinced them to do so. Remember that attorney who promised to fight for your rights? They probably convinced your spouse to ask for full custody or they relinquish their right to request it. The attorney convinced them that they need to preserve their rights. While there is truth to that statement, it is not definitive. The two of you will have plenty of opportunities to negotiate throughout the divorce proceedings. If, at the end of the day, you both sign a **consent agreement** giving you and your ex-spouse joint custody, the judge will not refuse to sign the final order of divorce because they asked for full custody in their complaint. The take-home point, however, is that this is an example of how an attorney can mangle your agreements and foster distrust by "advocating" to protect their client's rights.

Finally, if you are in a marriage where your spouse keeps threatening divorce, understand this is a form of emotional abuse designed to keep you under control. The message is, "If you don't behave, I'll leave and take everything!" This person may not really want a divorce but the only way they know how to interact is to control you. I know of several people whose spouses repeatedly threatened divorce. Eventually, tired of living with unrelenting uncertainty, they filed the complaint themselves. This unleashed tremendous rage in their spouses who had not anticipated that response. They had expected submission. Many people with personality disorders are incapable of understanding the consequences of their actions and are shocked to have put something into motion they cannot then control. They are genuinely astonished when they push a boulder down a hill, and it gathers speed.

If this is your situation, it is important to begin shifting the balance of power. Your spouse has been threatening you, or belittling you, for a while. They do it because it works. You have probably given in to them – perhaps to preserve the peace or simply to shush them – enough that they understand they can win simply by being persistent. They win because they endure the conflict longer than you. Their threat of divorce is a strategic move. They are "upping the ante" to get something from you, believing that your fear of disrupting you family will cause you to capitulate. If *you* file for divorce, however, you have "accepted" the "threat" and made it your own. You have stolen their thunder.

Now that they no longer have anything to threaten you with, they will be incredibly angry. Will they still threaten to take the children and the money? Will they now blame you for destroying the marriage? Sure, but that is old news. They have been doing that forever. Prepare yourself and figuratively – or literally – tell them to "talk to the hand." Their lawyer can work these things out with your lawyer. Know that they still expect you to capitulate as you have in the past. They will continue to threaten, but now you are taking control.

One way to begin shifting the balance of power is to ask for full custody of your children. You have nothing to lose – they are already furious. And you know they will probably share legal custody with you and have parenting time, so you are not "taking" anything from him. Trust in your own benevolence and morality, knowing you will make the right decision for yourself and your children when the time comes. But, for now, establish new ground rules by letting your spouse know that the ultimate threat of divorce is no longer something they can hold over your head.

BUYER'S REMORSE

A failed marriage *is* a sad thing, especially if there are children involved. It is natural after filing for divorce to have buyer's remorse. This is especially true if you are a person who likes pleasing others. You may think "if only:"

"If only I had tried harder."

"If only I had done it differently."

"If only I were nicer, kinder, more attractive ..."

But if you are thinking about everything you could have done differently so that they would have treated you better, then accept there is *nothing* you could have done. Your spouse's reactions are *independent* of you. You cannot "make" them yell or threaten you. They choose to do that. If trying harder to do things differently had been successful, then would not the two of you be in a vastly different place now? You might still be getting divorced, but the process would be much different.

Imagine the "perfect" divorce – if there is such a thing. Imagine the two of you sitting by the fireplace, quietly and sadly acknowledging that things had not worked out. You would talk at length, working *together* to ensure that both you and your children receive what each need. Your definition of "fair" would be similar. That is not the case if your spouse uses the threat of divorce to control or gain something from you. That is not a dialogue. And they are not a person who shares your definition of "fair."

It took me a while, but eventually I learned I had as much luck talking to a brick wall as I had talking to my ex-husband. Because he refused to listen, I learned there was nothing I could say. He had to make the choice not to hear me. In the same way, your spouse must make the choice to hear you. If they choose not to, then saying it differently or trying harder to explain yourself will accomplish nothing. You might as well talk to a brick wall.

TELLING THE KIDS

Many books advise people how to tell their kids that their parents are divorcing. Most include telling the children together, assuring them the divorce is not their fault, acknowledging everyone is sad, and reassuring them they are still loved.

In high-conflict cases, telling the kids together is not always possible. Recently, my children showed me an online video of two parents preparing to tell their children they were divorcing. The mother began by letting them know that she and their father had something important to say. Before she could explain further, however, their father burst out, "We're giving you a five dollar raise in your allowance." My children found this video funny because they understood that the father was positioning himself to look good. He had lied and manipulated his wife. He had trapped her. Were she to tell the kids now, after he had built their excitement about the promised raise in their allowance, *she* would be the "bad guy." The children would always remember that crucial moment in their lives when their father promised them something wonderful, only to have their joy crushed by their mother's terrible news.

You cannot count on your abusive spouse to cooperate with you when telling the children. The father in the above story demonstrated his willingness to use the children to hurt his wife. Without doubt, he will continue doing so throughout the divorce, no matter how many years it lasts. Even if your personality-disordered spouse does cooperate with you in telling the children, the moment the words are spoken you will be flung into the enemy camp. Whereas during your marriage they might have controlled your behavior by accusing you of hurting them or the family, now they will manipulate every interaction to validate your enemy status. Do not doubt that the children will be sacrificial pawns in their game of chess.

Your damage control should begin immediately. You must always be "on your children's side" no matter how long it takes. One conversation with the children will not suffice. Divorce is the death of their family, and they will need time to mourn. If you waiver in your support, you risk a small fissure through which your ex-spouse can burrow and further divide you from your children.

Children experience the five stages of grief at different times and for different lengths of time. Coping does not occur in nice, predictable stages but often cycles back and forth through these different emotions. Be prepared to help your children by tolerating their emotional upheaval. Do not "react" to it. Manage it.

To a child, divorce is the destruction of life as they know it. They will no longer have unlimited access to their parents. They may be forced to change homes and schools. They may lose friends and relatives, and their financial security will diminish. They must also cope with their parents' conflicts regarding visitation and custody. These are huge stresses for children and the way a child copes often depends on their age and support systems. Research indicates that younger children may have more immediate adjustment problems, but older children and adolescents may have more long-term effects. Infants are sensitive to the intensity and degree of conflict in the home and will respond with anxiety. This means they may cry without the ability to soothe and have difficulty sleeping. Preschool children tend to blame themselves. Their limited cognitive development prevents them from accurately interpreting events, including their own role in the divorce process. Many young children regress or stop maturing. Schoolchildren often feel anxious and depressed, which in turn affects their school and social behavior. Older children and adolescents also experience pain and anger, but many have the cognitive maturity to understand the reasons for divorce.

While most children recover from the initial shock of divorce within a year, parental support is essential to children's divorce adjustment. You can help your children by supporting them as they experience *their* divorce. It is imperative to be sensitive to the fact *your* divorce is not the same experience as *their* divorce. They will experience the disruption of their lives differently, worrying, naturally, about themselves. Like most people, they will fear the unknown, not knowing what their life will look like after the divorce. Recognize your children are helpless in the face of their parents' divorce and that feeling of helplessness contributes to their discomfort. Even if your child professes to understand that the divorce is necessary, they may still be angry with you for disrupting *their* life. You need to provide your child with the certainty that you are walking beside him as *they* experience this transition.

Be your child's safe harbor. That is, you must accept all your child's feelings, no matter how negative or hurtful they are. If your child is acting out on those feelings by behaving inappropriately, all negative feelings must be tolerated. They will feel less alone if they can tell you they hate you for ruining their life. It is hard, certainly, but imagine if they did not confess and harbored those feelings until they were old enough to walk away. By unconditionally accepting your child's feelings you are letting them know that you *hear* them. You are still the parent if you can soothe their temper tantrums.

By teaching your child that hurt and anger are as acceptable a part of them as their joy, you are teaching your child to tolerate themself. This, in turn, will help them tolerate the situation and feel less shame. Shame is humiliation plus guilt. Those children who feel responsible for their parent's divorce are prone to feeling shame. Others feel it simply because they were born into a family that could not keep itself together. They are part of something that failed.

Although divorce is prevalent and not as much of a stigma as it once was, the paradigm remains that a two heterosexual-parent family is the gold standard. Children sense that their family is not "what it is supposed to be." Regardless of how much you try to normalize your children's' new family structure, they are still exposed to the outside world, which idolizes the intact family. Besides supporting them, you can also help them adjust by **teaching them to fail.** Teach them that failure is a misnomer and is really a chance for a "do-over," but with newly acquired knowledge. Learning to fail simply means that Plan A did not work out – it often does not – but there is always a Plan B. Although the failure of Plan A is a monumental event, normalizing the fact that not everything works out according to plan may help them view the world through a different lens, which may, in turn, smooth their adjustment to their parents' divorce.

Families are systems and members interact with one another in verbal and nonverbal ways. They respond to each other's words and body language. They respond to each other's silence. They respond to their own thoughts about the other person. Once family patterns are established, they tend to be self-perpetuating. Your divorce is not an insular event. Each family member will have a unique emotional and behavioral reaction to the divorce and the ensuing consequences. Like the chicken and the egg, each behavior causes a behavioral response, which, in turn, causes another behavior response, and so on. Social spheres, employment, and educational institutions are not free from impact either. For example, a 10-year-old child who acts out in school will stress their parent because they must now miss work to meet with the guidance counselor, resulting in stress in the workplace and additional stress in the family. Sensing this, the 8-year-old sibling might refuse to go to sleep that evening. Despite your exhaustion, arguing about their bedtime that night is not, in the scheme of things, advantageous to any of you. Instead, admit that the situation is difficult on both and work *together* to develop a compromise. You will spend less time and energy talking than yelling, and the children will be more likely to go to bed feeling that you had their back, rather than being the enemy.

Only you know what is normal for your children. Some children manage change better than others. Some children manage fear and uncertainty better than others. Watch for signs that your children are struggling. Monitor their grades. Keep track of their friendships and activities. You know what your child needs. Perhaps your child needs therapy or a healthy outlet such as kickboxing. Perhaps meditation or yoga will help. Whatever you provide for your child externally, it is not as important as what you provide directly. Children need you to consistently be there for them. They need limit setting and support to protect their sense of security. Being their stable, safe haven will go a long way in helping the entire family adjust.

CHAPTER FIVE:

Divorces involving minor children can take from six months to more than two years. While there have been efforts to reduce the time between the filing of the **complaint** and entering the **final judgment of divorce**, attorneys and therapists generally agree that a family needs time to adjust and transition from being intact to divorced. From a legal perspective, custody and parenting time must be determined. Property and debt must be allocated. And because divorce is a court action, complicated court rules apply that are designed to preserve the rights of both parties.

During the period between filing the complaint and entry of the final judgment, the rules the family lived by no longer apply. Decisions must be made, such as when each parent will spend time with the children and who will pay the mortgage and car loan. The anger and hurt that accompanies a divorce make it difficult for couples to resolve these issues together. Furthermore, while spouses are both transitioning from identifying as a couple to identifying as a single person – no easy task in itself – they will not do it at the same time. Often each person cycles through a myriad of emotions. There will be moments when one person still processes a problem as a couple while the other is processing the same issue as a single person. And vice versa. This heightens the sense of abandonment and hurt.

The situation becomes more challenging when one party moves out of the house, or if one party wants the other to leave. They may seek an order asking to exclude their spouse from the family home, although often they must demonstrate that physical or emotional harm is likely to occur. Regardless of how a person ends up leaving the martial home, that person will be disinclined to want to pay the rent on both their apartment *and* the mortgage on the marital home. Nor will they want to pay two sets of utility bills. But this parent will want to spend time with the children.

In addition to deciding who lives where, concerns about depletion of the marital assets often arise. Even after the complaint for divorce is filed, both spouses have equal access to their money. That means either spouse can empty an account. Access is restricted only after the judge enters an order preventing both parties from spending any money other than what is needed for ordinary expenses. This is often in the form of a **restraining order** prohibiting you and your spouse from spending money outside of the ordinary course of business. This **temporary order** will apply until the final judgment of divorce is entered (signed by the judge). Failure to abide by the order may result in a **contempt of court** charge.

If you are concerned that your spouse will drain the accounts or stop paying their share of the bills, you may take a portion of the marital money – no more than half – before such an order is entered. Deposit the money into an account that only you can access. But be open about it. Let both your spouse and the judge know that you did this to preserve marital assets and prevent your spouse from disposing of them. Do not spend the money unless you must. If your spouse fails to pay the mortgage and you do not have enough to pay it yourself, then use that money. Keep an accounting of what you spent and why, that way your former spouse cannot accuse you of stealing.

Because decisions must be made about each parent's access to the children and how the household will be maintained during the lengthy divorce process, the judge may enter several **temporary orders**. These might include a schedule outlining when each parent may spend time with the children. This is often called a **temporary parenting plan**. In a high-conflict divorce, it is likely the temporary orders will be violated. A narcissistic personality-disordered spouse does not believe the rules apply to them. A borderline personality-disordered spouse may interpret the order so rigidly or in such as skewed way that their logic defies common sense. For example, Heather's parenting plan provided that the children would be with each parent during the Thanksgiving Day holiday on alternate years. The first year, the children were with Heather. Although her ex-husband had parenting time on Wednesday nights, they remained with Heather on the evening before Thanksgiving and he picked them up on Friday for the beginning of his parenting time that weekend. The next year he collected the children at 3 p.m. after school on Wednesday for his Thanksgiving holiday with the children. At 3 p.m. on Thanksgiving Day, Heather arrived at his house and demanded the children. Her argument was that his Thanksgiving "Day" parenting time ended twenty-four hours after he picked the children up from school. Heather and her ex-husband returned to court to determine what a "day" meant. Heather lost. The judge ruled that the Thanksgiving Day holiday was a twenty-four-hour period that began at 12:00 a.m. on Thursday and ended at 12:00 p.m. on Thursday.

It was not, as Heather argued, a twenty-four-hour period spanning Wednesday and Thursday.

In high-conflict cases, temporary orders are commonplace because the parties have difficulty working together. Although designed to be temporary and last only the duration of the divorce proceedings, these orders can trap the parties into a permanent arrangement. Temporary can easily become permanent.

It is widely accepted that children need stability and consistency. Because of that, temporary orders can create a big trap. If the divorce proceedings last too long, one parent may convince the court that the temporary parenting plan should be permanent because the children have adapted to it and changing it would be destabilizing. Imagine that your ex-spouse, who has moved out of the house, files a motion for temporary orders. The judge's order establishes a parenting time arrangement with which you are unhappy. Perhaps there is too much "back and forth" for the children or too many overnights at an unfamiliar home. You express your concerns to your attorney, but they advise you not to worry because "it is only temporary." But your divorce lasts 18 months and the children have adjusted to the schedule. Do you disrupt it? Does the judge? The answer is likely to be no because the notion that children need stability is so prevalent in our society. Now your temporary situation has become permanent.

Kristen had moved out of her marital home and was living at a friend's house. She believed it was important for her son to have stability, so she and her ex-husband agreed their son would remain at home with his father. Every afternoon, when school ended, Kristen would return "home" to help her son with his homework, make his dinner, and put him to bed. Then she returned to her friend's home.

This temporary arrangement sounds very child-centered but could easily have deteriorated. Her ability to come and go from her marital home was dependent on her ex-husband's good graces. If they had a conflict, he could have banned her from the home. Because Kristin had not provided a home for her son, the court may have seen this as evidence that she is *not* child-centered and severely limited her parenting time or even denied her custody.

The take-home point is that "temporary" might not be temporary. It could become permanent. Your task, then, is to begin crafting a parenting plan schedule early on. It is extremely difficult because you are struggling with so many issues at once and plotting when you will *not* see your children feels counter intuitive. Although you and your family will be living in a state of chaos during the initial stages of your divorce, do not rush to have orders entered.

Instead, maximize your time with your children and collect affidavits from those teachers and coaches supporting your claim that you are the primary parent. Consider a plan that is in your children's best interests. Recognize that the court will grant your ex-spouse time with the kids, but if you believe they are abusive, do not attack them as a way of limiting their time. The court will not want to hear it at this early stage of the game (if ever). Instead, speak of the parenting you do. Explain to the court the routines you and your children have established and that are successful. Emphasize the other parent's absence from those rituals. And then discuss why you believe overnights are not in your children's best interests. Perhaps your daughter is on the swim team and needs to get up extremely early, something that is difficult for her, but the morning routine is something you have always managed. You and your daughter have developed a routine that works. If your ex-spouse argues that they can manage that situation, your counter argument should be that this would be very unstable for your daughter in an already unstable situation. Then suggest that their other parent have the evening with your daughter and return her at bedtime. This way, you explain, they have quality time together and your sleepy daughter can maintain her difficult morning routine.

The focus of your argument, then, is on your daughter's needs and how you have been managing them all her life. By focusing on your relationship with your daughter and the special routine you have developed to help her manage, you are appealing to the judge's sensibility that stability is important for children's well-being.

Keep records. Record when your children are picked up and returned. Is your former spouse always late? If so, note it. Do your children get to school on time? If not, note it. How are they doing in school? Are they clean when they return or does the other parent fail to enforce hygiene rules? What have your children been eating? If your children do well, then try to be happy that their other parent is rising to the challenge. If not, you will have evidence to support your challenge to this arrangement.

A common temporary order is a **personal protection order (PPO).** If a person feels unsafe, if they have been threatened or stalked, they may ask the judge to enter an order preventing their oppressor from approaching them. Proof must be presented. A judge will not enter a PPO unless they are presented with documentation, including specific facts such as police reports, medical records, and emails. Even if the judge is convinced, however, the PPO is usually temporary until the other party is served and has an opportunity to appear in court and present their defense. After the hearing, the judge may either extend the PPO for a finite period (usually a year or for the duration of the divorce) or vacate it.

Protection orders provide some comfort, but they, too, are a double-edged sword. Despite the order preventing your ex-spouse from being within a specified number of feet from you, you will still need to communicate with them. School, scheduling, and other child-related issues still need to be decided. You still need to exchange the children. If your child is still an infant, the handover will have to be person to person. When there are protection orders, the exchange is often held at the local police station, which is uncomfortable for everyone, including the children. Some parents elect to exchange the children at McDonald's but that quickly gets old. I know of one couple who exchanged their children at an exit ramp off the side of the highway. Protective orders are inconvenient when children are involved.

Your ex-spouse is likely to abide by the terms of the protective order at the beginning, perhaps for the first few weeks, but eventually its inconvenience becomes cumbersome for both of you. Often the parents begin communicating. It seems illogical not to. The problem arises when your former spouse gets too comfortable and reverts to their old abusive ways. If you return to court to enforce the order, they may successfully argue that you violated your own order and have waived its protection. You will have lost your credibility.

BEWARE OF CONTINUANCES

A **continuance** is a delay. Most attorneys will agree to a continuance when asked by opposing counsel. It is a courtesy. They are looking ahead to a time when they might need the same courtesy. But continuances can harm *you*. They give the other party more time to prepare and cost you time, money, and stress.

When Sarah filed for divorce, a hearing date was set on her motion for temporary orders. Her husband's attorney asked for a continuance, and it was granted. Three weeks later, when they arrived in court, he was armed with half a dozen affidavits supporting his claim for custody. He used that time wisely. She was blindsided.

Kristen was in the middle of her divorce and had already filed two motions asking the judge to order her husband to pay for the children's activities and medical expenses. This was her third motion because while her husband had paid some of what he owed; he never paid it all. She also had learned that what he did pay was taken from the children's college accounts. At the hearing, his attorney asked for a continuance. He offered what Kristen considered a lame excuse, something about him not having had enough time to review the invoices she had sent. Kristen was certain the judge would see through this obvious delay tactic. But shockingly, the judge agreed to the third delay. You can imagine her frustration. Her costs: her attorney's time preparing for and attending the hearing; her attorney's time preparing for and attending the next hearing; and her out-of-pocket cost for solely paying for the children's activities and medical expenses that their father should have been sharing.

Unfortunately, when the judge rules on a matter like this, nothing can be done. But you can tell your attorney you do not agree. If you suspect your former spouse is asking for a continuance for illegitimate reasons, tell your attorney, "No." Your attorney may think you are being thoughtless, but you are paying your attorney to represent you, not to like you.

MOTIONS IN FAMILY COURT

The mechanism for asking a judge to enter an order during the divorce is a **motion**. Motions are formal requests to the judge and are usually presented in a **pleading**, which is a structured document whose components are dictated by court rules. Motions are frequently accompanied by **affidavits** or **declarations** – sworn witness statements – and **briefs** or **memoranda**, which explain to the judge why the asking party (the movant) is legally entitled to receive what they are asking for.[5] Motions in a divorce can ask for anything from increasing or reducing child support, to allowing a child to attend a birthday party. Whenever a divorcing couple is unable to resolve an issue themselves, they may ask the judge to decide for them via a motion.

Motions in family law court differ from motions in other types of litigation. In other civil and criminal cases, most motions are about legal issues, such as a request to exclude the opposing party's expert witness. In family law, the motions are about family issues. They are personal. When couples are divorcing, they often file motions to resolve key issues such as parenting time, child support, and spousal support.

In high-conflict cases, couples become **Motion Frequent-Flyers**. Because the parents cannot or will not agree on even simple matters, the court becomes the forum of choice. Motions are filed to resolve

---

5 The legal brief contains legal argument supporting the movant's request. The affidavit is a statement, signed and sworn, that verifies facts alleged in the brief. For example, if the motion states that on, "November 21, Plaintiff/Counter-Defendant was observed returning home unable to stand upright, with messy clothes and alcohol on his breath," then the affidavit will state: "I, Defendant/Counter-Plaintiff, observed Plaintiff/Counter-Defendant return home on the evening of November 21. He was unable to stand upright, his clothes were in disarray, and I smelled alcohol on his breath." The affidavit, then, provides the factual support for the claims made by the movant.

minor issues such as adjusting holiday schedules, telephone access to children in the other parent's home, and other day-to-day details of parenting plan implementation. Because you are likely to be in court often, asking the judge to resolve mundane issues, the chances of the judge concluding that both you and your ex-spouse are difficult and unreasonable, is extremely high. That is why it is so important to begin establishing your **Courtroom Persona** early on. You want the judge to understand that your ex-spouse is the real problem. Not you.

Motions are also filed to harass or bankrupt you. Every time your ex-spouse files a motion, you must respond to the motion, the accompanying affidavit, and the brief. You must also appear at the hearing. If you do not, the judge will award your ex-spouse what they asked for. Having your attorney represent you is costly. They must consult with you prior to preparing the pleadings and affidavits, consult with you again before the final draft is filed with the court, and attend the hearing, which can last for hours. Even though a hearing is scheduled to begin at 8:30 a.m., there may be an extensive line of cases before yours. You might not be able to present your case until 11:30 a.m. Attorneys charge by the hour. Responding to one motion may cost up to $10,000. Because your ex-spouse knows that taking you to court costs you time, money, and stress, it is a means of hurting you. A third reason motions are filed is for validation. You or your ex-spouse want the judge to understand the trauma you are experiencing at the hand of the other. You want the judge to punish them. The presenting issue in the motion might be to 'order Suzie's mother to allow me to take Suzie to my family reunion, which falls on her time.' But the underlying message is that Suzie's mother is unreasonable or irrational. That may be true, or it may be that the mother refused because of something the father did earlier. Perhaps he prevented her from fixing Suzie's hair before her dance recital – a ritual mother and daughter shared until the recital fell on his time. In addition to attending the family reunion, Suzie's father wants the judge to acknowledge that he is reasonable, and his ex-wife caused all their problems. Of course, she wants the same thing. But presenting this history to the judge can be counterproductive. The judge may not care why Suzie's mother refused, only that she did so. Suzie's mom, then, should present a stronger defense, such as explaining that the reunion falls on the same date as her own family event.

Another important thing to know about motions is that often, psychologically, the presenting problem is not the real problem. There are subconscious reasons your disordered ex-spouse continually files motions. Your disordered ex-spouse's need for validation is extremely deeply rooted and insatiable. They have spent a lifetime trying to silence those critical inner voices telling them that them that they are bad and unlovable. When you married, you validated them. You accepted them as the person they *wanted to be*. Your marriage was the ultimate validation of your disordered person's desired self-image. "They love me and therefore I must be a good person." But when you divorce – regardless of who initiated the divorce – you are rejecting that longed-for reality. In your disordered spouse's mind, you are telling them that you cannot love them because they are unlovable; that they are, in fact, the bad person they so deeply fear. And this is intolerable. Thus, they will do anything and use any resource at hand to prove themselves right and you wrong. Motions afford them an opportunity to be proven "right" and therefore, ultimately validated.

This is also why your disordered ex-spouse fights so viciously to win a motion. They "live for the fight" because for them it is a life-or-death struggle. The life they fight to save is their own distorted self-image. Death would be admitting that *your* image of them is true – and if you win the motion then you might be right about them. And this is also why your ex-spouse lies with impunity. Their lies are created to support their distorted self-image. As soon as the words escape their mouth, they believe them. They instantaneously become their reality. And in that new reality, they are unequivocally right, and you are unequivocally wrong. This revisionist history is like truth handed down to them by God, and they will fight to have that truth validated by the judge. It is imperative that their lie – or new reality – is accepted by the rest of the world. To make that happen, they consume that reality and express it to the world with such remarkable sincerity and conviction that everyone around them believes it, too. Even you may doubt your own reality – how you remember a past event – and often you will find yourself needing a "reality check" from friends and family.

Parents in high-conflict divorces are often caught up in a Catch-22 cycle, reacting to real or perceived hurts by creating more real or perceived hurts. Catch-22 came from the book with the same name written by Joseph Heller. It defines "circular reasoning." The solution to a problem is impossible to achieve because that solution is inherent in the problem itself. The problem has no beginning and no end. In the same way your conflict had no beginning and no end. It was a series of actions and reactions. You want to end the conflict that gave rise to the motion, you want to protect yourself and your children, but you must respond and remain engaged in the conflict to protect yourself and your children. It is a vicious cycle. And sadly, no judge deciding on a motion to allow Suzie to attend a family reunion will ever fully understand this destructive dynamic.

You must remember that in family court neither you nor your ex-spouse are likely to be validated. The judge does not care about either parents deeply rooted psychological issues or even why Suzie's mother refused her ex-husband's request. The judge only wants the matter resolved.

When Sarah changed her son's bar mitzvah date without consulting the father who had married a Christian woman and no longer practiced Judaism, he filed a motion asking the judge that he be allowed to participate in fifty percent of the bar mitzvah events, including attending the private and expensive party Sarah was hosting. He wanted the judge to punish Sarah. When she tried explaining that she had not consulted her ex-husband because he no longer practiced Judaism and he unilaterally removed their son from religious school, the judge did not care. She was only interested in hearing the immediate story, not the background. The judge observed that a bar mitzvah is a big event, and a child is entitled to have both parents present. She ruled that the father, his wife, and his stepchildren all may participate in the bar mitzvah events, including Sarah's private party. Sarah tried arguing that her ex-husband could host his own party for *his* family and friends, but the judge did not want to hear that either. Her anger at Sarah implied that she found Sarah selfish. Sarah had damaged her **Courtroom Persona**.

Judges are overworked and do not have the time to consider the complexities and interpersonal dynamics between divorcing couples. They do not have time to review all the events leading up to that moment. The judge can only see the snapshot of events presented to them inside their courtroom. The judge in Sarah's case is not interested in *why* Sarah excluded her ex-husband from the bar mitzvah events. She only saw that Sarah did something "bad." Unfortunately for Sarah, the snapshot of her life that the judge was exposed to was Sarah's reaction to a series of painful events. The judge concluded that in this instance Sarah was, in fact, trying to alienate the children from their father. The next time he and Sarah are in court, the judge will review the file and see only that she had to order Sarah not to exclude her ex-husband from their son's bar mitzvah. She will not remember any history that led up to that event. Thus, when the next issue comes before her, the judge will address it from the lingering perspective that Sarah is the unreasonable parent.

It is imperative to remember that the judge only sees your reaction to an event. It is that reaction your ex-spouse brings before the judge in the form of a motion, asking the judge to *order* you to be reasonable. Your ex-spouse may have knowingly or unknowingly provoked you but the chances of you successfully explaining why you made the choice that brought you to court, are slim. All the judge will see is that you behaved inappropriately in response to a reasonable request from your ex-spouse. It hurts. It is terrorism. Imagine a terrorist organization that executes men from a village. The terrorists are husbands and sons from a nearby village. When the survivors from the first village retaliate, the terrorists videotape them storming their village and killing indiscriminately because all the men are clutching their wives and mothers. These women are killed, too, and their murder is posted on the Internet. World opinion will condemn the killing of the women and will not excuse it because the murder was in retaliation for the initial attack.

Your ex-spouse uses these terrorist tactics, and it is *extremely difficult* not to react to them. Your choices must be made in a vacuum, independent of what they did to provoke you. Ideally, Sarah should have invited her ex-husband to participate in the bar mitzvah planning, regardless of how painful that would be. Chances are that he really would not be interested. She knew that when she made the choice to exclude him, but by making the choice for him, she woke the proverbial sleeping giant. Now that he was aware that she wanted to exclude him, his disordered personality would not permit her to do so. He would not tolerate her exposure of her reality, that he had abandoned his religion, and instantaneously revised history. In his mind, he was still an active Jewish father. Sarah's ex-husband filed the motion because he wanted to prove his reality. He succeeded because in a vacuum his request seemed reasonable. He was also adept at portraying himself as the *charming victim* and Sarah as the *evil oppressor*.

Choose your battles wisely. Step back and decide whether you need to file a motion to resolve the matter, whether you need to answer their motion by fighting, or whether the issue needs to be resolved at all. Think long-term. If they are asking the court to allow them to take the children to their family reunion on your time, even though you have already said no, once they file the **motion** in court, you can always change your mind. Do not allow yourself to get drawn into the battle simply because they fired a shot across your bow. Consider, instead, that agreeing to their request after they file a motion might benefit you. First, they may drop the motion rather than spend more money at a hearing. Now you have saved yourself time and money. And you have reacted in a way they did not anticipate. This makes you *unpredictable*, which should cause them to think twice before "wasting money" filing another motion.

Second, before agreeing you can ask for something in return, perhaps some of their parenting time. Even if you offered that earlier and they refused, their attorney is now involved and likely to advise them to agree. Even unscrupulous attorneys understand that going to court after the other party agrees will make their client appear unreasonable. And finally, if you do end up in court, you can play that "reasonable" card. You can calmly explain to the court that you attempted to work out a compromise but that your ex-spouse rejected it. Will the judge want to hear that you did not agree until after the motion was filed? Perhaps, but the judge will be more interested in settling the matter and moving on to the next case.

Should you choose to agree to your ex-spouse's request before they file a motion, remember that you are not likely to build a "bank account" of good will. Test this hypothesis once. In high-conflict cases, there usually is no bank account. Gary never remembered the requests he had agreed to. He immediately wiped the record clean. Nor did he "remember" the terrible things he did that hurt his ex-wife. Instead, like all personality-disordered people, he only remembered her *reaction*, which he then exploited in court to prove her wickedness. It is this cycle of action – reaction – new action that results in high-conflict couples becoming **Motion Frequent-Flyers**. You must learn to respond to all your ex-spouse's parenting requests in a vacuum, as if nothing had ever happened between the two of you. You must function as if you were strangers.

Another factor to consider is that filing a motion to resolve a parenting issue is not always about the subject matter of the motion. It is also about making a power play. Your ex-spouse will use motions for that purpose and so can you. Filing puts them on the defensive, shifting the burden of proof by requiring *them* to prove that their refusal of your reasonable request was, in fact, reasonable. Another advantage of filing – and do not do it too often – is that it demonstrates that you are unpredictable. If you file motions irregularly, your ex-spouse will never be certain which of their actions you will contest and which you will not. By being unpredictable, they learn that old rules (when you were married) do not apply. If they are less certain how you will respond, they are more likely to think twice before relying on their old bullying tactics.

Should you consider filing a motion, however, chose wisely. Some issues really are not worth fighting about. Some issues, such as your children's safety, are. Before you file a motion or respond to a motion, consider whether you are acting in anger or if your concerns are legitimate. If your primary motivation is anger, then strategize whether you should proceed and if so, how will it further your cause.

Finally, one of the many problems with **motions** is that the facts alleged in both the **motion** and **affidavit** are the author's narrative. They tell the story from their perspective. Your personality-disordered spouse sees the world only through their eyes and their vision is distorted. Additionally, they are capable of instantaneously re-writing history to cast themselves in the role of victim. So, although people are sworn to tell the truth when they submit affidavits or declarations, the reality is that disordered people lie. They exaggerate the truth and manipulate the facts. They develop false memories. Dan's ex-wife refused to tell him the date and times of the children's doctor and dentist appointments.

Dan wanted to be there but no matter how often he asked, she refused to tell him when the appointments were. Yet, in an affidavit to the court, she stated under oath that her husband, the children's stepfather, had to hold her son's hand at the dentist while getting a filling because Dan was not available. In the world Dan's ex-wife created in her motion and affidavit, Dan was unavailable for their son. Her attorney, of course, accepted this story as true without question. In court he created an image that made Dan's ex-wife, her new husband, and the children appear as a happy family. Dan was cast as the intruder. The lawyer did their job and created a positive narrative, which Dan felt obligated to dispel. Dan won his right to be notified of the children's medical appointments – a right he already had because he shared legal custody with his ex-wife – but in doing so, he, like Sarah, lost ground in the larger battle. Not only was his **Court Persona** diminished, but his ex-wife knew exactly how to make Dan squirm. All she needed was a picture of her perfect "new family."

Dan needed to be stoic, to adopt an attitude of concerned indifference, and focus only on the presenting issue. As difficult as this is, remember that once upon a time you accepted the world as your ex-spouse saw it. You did so because it was necessary to survive in your marriage. An abused spouse often adapts by accepting the abusing spouse's view of the world. If, for example, the abusing spouse states that a neighbor was rude at a neighborhood picnic, the abused spouse learns to accept that. They will not defend the neighbor even if they believe their spouse's interpretation of the event was inaccurate.[6]

---

6 Some people might agree simply because they do not care, but an abused spouse will deny their own feelings — perhaps they liked the neighbors and hoped that they would become friends — to avoid the conflict.

That would generate an argument. As time passes, the abused spouse begins accepting their abuser's viewpoint and adopts it as their own. They look at the world through their abuser's distorted lens. Having done that during the years of their marriage, Dan could certainly revive that "role" and "act" that way again, at least for the few hours he was in court. The **Courtroom Persona** Dan should have presented was, "I recognize how nice it is for my children's stepfather to be there for him, but wouldn't it be in their best interests for their biological dad to be there, too?" Unless Dan is a felony sex offender – which he was not – no judge is going to deny him that reasonable request.

PREPARING YOUR PRIVATE RESPONSE

When you receive your ex-spouse's motion you will experience stress and anxiety. These emotions are enhanced if the motion is filled with lies and outrageous demands. The first thing to do after you read it is to put it aside and do something for yourself. Go to the gym. Call a friend for a *reality check*. Take a hot shower and curl up with a good book. The important thing is to take a moment to breathe.

Prepare yourself for the next time you must read the offending document. Select a time and place where you will not be disturbed for an hour. You may want to copy the document or print out a second so that you have one clean one for your records, and another for writing notes. Arm yourself with pen and paper, too. Then begin to respond to each factual misstatement you read. You can be as angry as you want in this version because it will not be the response you provide your lawyer. This is your cathartic moment when you can spew as much venom as you want, knowing that no one will ever see it.

Aside from helping yourself feel better, this exercise also helps you:

- ❖ Identify the incorrect facts.
- ❖ Outline your truths.
- ❖ Identify and prioritize which wrongful accusations need to be refuted.
- ❖ Begin the process of strategizing how to prepare your response.

Make certain to correspond your responses to the numbered paragraphs in the motion and accompanying affidavit.[7] For example, suppose your ex-wife files a motion asking for more child support, claiming that you waste your money on alcohol and are always drunk when you pick up the children from her house. Your notes may state:

> LINE NUMBER SIX: Not true. I do go out on Saturday nights when I am not with the kids and have had an occasional drink, but no more than two at any given time. My wife is strongly opposed to any alcohol and has a distorted notion of what "too much" drinking is. I pay all the household bills and other than going out every other Saturday night (primarily to a restaurant or movie), the only money I have spent on myself is rent for my apartment. After our child was born my wife quit her job

---

7 Motions, like all legal pleadings, are written so that each sentence is a separate numbered paragraph. This is so that the defendant, when answering, can refer to each enumerated paragraph, making it easier for all parties to track what is and what is not contested.

without discussing it with me, even though we had arranged for childcare. She now complains she has no money and no time to go out with her friends and is using this motion to extort money from me.

Now do the same for the brief. Write your private response. But while the **motion** and **affidavit** are written in enumerated paragraphs, the **brief** is not. You will have to develop a system to correspond your notes with the allegations you are refuting. One way is to use an alphabetical or numerical system. Number each lie or misstatement directly on the page, and then on a separate page, write your factual response. For example:

Page Two

Brief in Support

On the evening of November 21, movant was home with her daughter who was sleeping in her bedroom. Movant was quietly watching television when __ burst into the house. Movant could smell the alcohol on his breath from across the room .... [1]

Your Response:

[1] BRIEF PAGE TWO: I did not "burst" through the door. I used my key. I finished my beer two hours before I got home, so there is no way she could smell alcohol on my breath. Also, she was talking on the phone when I came home, and she went into the kitchen so I could not hear her conversation.

When you have finished, you will have a complete record of your truths. From there, you can begin preparing your **actual response.**

DRAFTING THE ACTUAL RESPONSE

It is natural to want to defend yourself and refute each false accusation to preserve your good name, but how you do it involves careful strategizing.

❖ Should you, for example, admit to having a few drinks that night, but state it was only two?

❖ Should you defend the allegation that you are an alcoholic?

❖ Do you attack your wife's unreasonable and intractable position about alcohol?

❖ Do you discuss the fact that money has been a problem since she quit her job without discussing the matter?

❖ Do you discuss how she is angry that you moved into an apartment because now there is even less money?

❖ Do you discuss how you made the decision to move into an apartment because she has made the situation at home so uncomfortable and hostile?

❖ Do you discuss what she has done to make the situation so uncomfortable and hostile?

Think about it: so many questions generated by a few lines in a motion. And none of these addresses the *real* issue, that she wants more money, money you do not believe she deserves. Start with and focus on the core issue. Do not allow yourself to get distracted by the mud she is slinging.

Begin your **response** with an acknowledgment that she is attempting to distract the judge with unsubstantiated allegations. (Other than her own account, she has no evidence of your alleged alcoholism.) Then suggest to the judge that you prefer to focus on her *real* agenda, which is her effort to extort more money from you. Next, defend your position with evidence. Provide an accounting of all the money you have paid to your ex-wife. Include copies of canceled checks and statements showing that bills were paid. Add a budget of what her reasonable expenses are. If there is a surplus, point that out. You can even ask the court to enter an order reducing the amount you pay. Keep the judge's attention focused on the issue and not the mud.

Once you have thoroughly addressed the issue, you can spend a brief sentence or two refuting the allegations. Do it in broad strokes. You do not want to get yourself caught in a "he-said-she-said" argument about every alleged fact. Review that first response you drafted and select the most compelling misstatement. Think about why it angers you. Is it because it is true or because she mischaracterized your ordinary and reasonable behavior? Is it reflective of the problems you experienced in your marriage – that she is rigid and intractable? Next, consider how you will respond. You may:

❖ Summarily dismiss the allegations as unsubstantiated because there is no proof.

❖ Summarily attack them for their rigidity, noting that when you were married, she sat with you when you occasionally enjoyed a single beer.

❖ Attack her further by suggesting that her rigidity has created issues between her and the children.

No matter which response you choose, retain control over the situation by refusing to allow yourself to get caught up in the argument.

Your objective is to raise the issue and then drop it just as quickly. In this way, you acknowledge that they are mudslinging, but let the court know you are above the fray. Is this approach guaranteed to work? No, but it is far better to appear reasonable, rational, and responsive to the *real issue* than to allow yourself to get trapped in the mudslinging.

DISCOVERY

Before trial, each party to a legal action may access information belonging to their opponent. Each party seeks information that will either support or defend their position. This process, called **discovery**, applies in divorce cases as well. When a couple divorces, the marital estate (the sum of their property minus their debt) must be divided. To do this, the value of the property must also be determined, and the amount of marital debt must be quantified. If the parties cannot agree, the judge will decide. But before any final decisions are reached, each party must value the property and debt and **discover** what value the other person gives that same item.

Marital property belongs to both spouses. It is comprised of property acquired during the marriage and includes real property (the home) and personal property such as cars, furniture, and investments. During marriage, each spouse is legally entitled to access all financial information relating to marital property to determine its value. Often, however, spouses do not possess or have access to all the information they need.

Busy couples typically divide and conquer. The husband may pay the monthly bills and the wife may manage the investments. If these transactions occur online, they are likely to be password protected. In a marriage where the spouses are particularly busy, where they are not close, or where one spouse is personality disordered, passwords are not always shared. This becomes a problem when the divorcing couple is trying to value assets and debt and have no access to the account information. The wife may not know how much the monthly water bill is or if there is an abundance of credit card debt. The husband may not know the value of her retirement account.

There may also be private or secret accounts. Some people maintain private accounts that their spouses may or may not know about. Some people own businesses and do not want their spouses to have access to its finances. Or a person may deny their spouse access to financial information relating to property they believe belongs only to them. They may believe the property is **separate.**

Separate property is property acquired before the marriage, property that is inherited by either spouse, or property that is gifted to one of them. Separate property belongs to *either* the husband or the wife – not both – but only if the property remains separate. That is, if the person who acquired the property does not use it for the benefit of the marriage. If both the husband and wife use the separate property, it is said to be **commingled** and becomes marital property. For example, if Andrea inherits money from her deceased father and uses the money to buy a Mustang convertible that she and her husband Mike drive on the weekends, the convertible becomes a marital asset. Separate property must remain separate to maintain its separate status.

As a rule, married property is divided equally between the husband and wife, and separate property remains with the person who acquired it. This is not a rigid rule, however. Family court is a court of **equity** or fairness, and sometimes receiving fifty percent of the marital property is not deemed fair. Also, separate property may be invaded to equalize the financial outcome of the divorce. Suppose Andrea inherited $2 million from her father. Assume that the net total of Andrea and Mike's marital assets is $300,000. Ordinarily, Andrea and Mike would each receive $150,000 in the divorce, or fifty percent. But because Andrea would also have the money from her father, the court may either award Mike a greater percentage of the marital estate (more than fifty percent) or require that Andrea give some of her inherited money to Mike. As a court of **equity** or **fairness**, the court has the right to do this. Mike, then, is entitled to all financial information pertaining to Andrea's inheritance.

Another possibility is that the court may find that Andrea's inheritance was commingled. I have witnessed judges go to great lengths to reach this outcome in the interests of fairness. Once I was speaking to a judge who shared a story about a divorce in which the husband was an avid baseball fan. This man's hobby was to collect souvenirs from Major League Baseball Parks across the country. He displayed his collection in a room in the house where there was a couch and a television, and he and his wife would sit in that room and watch baseball games together. When they divorced, the husband claimed that the baseball collection was his separate property because he started the collection before the marriage and it was his hobby, not hers. The judge disagreed and ordered that the collection was marital property because both spouses enjoyed it. In my experience, then, judges are often generous in defining marital property.

If your ex-spouse possesses property that you anticipate they will wrongly claim is separate, do your best to commingle it. If Andrea and Mike did not drive her Mustang convertible on the weekends, but Andrea drove it to shop for the family's groceries, Mike should inform the court. She used the separate property for marital purposes. Similarly, if Andrea uses her separate money to pay for a vacation for her and her daughter to visit grandma in Florida, then Mike can make the argument that the "separate" money was commingled because it paid for their daughter's vacation. Mike is not guaranteed success, but he will certainly never have access to a share of that money if he does not try.

If Mike does not know exactly how much money Andrea inherited, or if he does not know how much is in her retirement account, he will have to acquire the information through the legal process of **discovery**. This requires him or his attorney to **subpoena** information, which is a court order demanding that the information be delivered to him. Like Mike, you may also serve **interrogatories** on your spouse, which are questions they must answer under oath. An interrogatory question might ask a party to list all financial accounts to which they have access, for example. If they exclude an account that you later discover, you can **impeach** them, which means exposing their lie to the judge.

Interrogatories are not used exclusively to collect financial information. They are used to understand your ex-spouse's position on custody, parenting time, and spousal support. Interrogatories help attain a realistic understanding of your ex-spouse's position and how they foresee the outcome of the divorce. Attorneys often send interrogatories to the other parent asking them to describe their preferred custody arrangement. Questions also often inquire about parenting responsibilities. Who wakes the children in the morning and feeds them breakfast? Which parent supervises homework? This information is then used to develop a custody arrangement and parenting plan. If your spouse had once threatened to take the children from you unless you complied with their demands, for example, they are unlikely to make the same threat when answering the interrogatory under oath. Your hope is that they answer the questions more realistically and propose a plan with which you can work. The plan might be balanced in their favor, but the judge or mediator will use it as a starting point, and you know that your ex-spouse will never get exactly what they want.

Interrogatories are also used to expose *faults* and *lies*. The recipient must answer truthfully, and if they do not, the lie will be exposed in court and undermine that person's credibility. Questions about a suspected affair or drug addictions, for example, if answered truthfully, *will* be used against an ex-spouse. If answered untruthfully, however, the ex-spouse will be impeached.

Because of the breadth and intrusiveness of **discovery,** people do not like responding to it. On the other hand, some use discovery as a legal strategy to harass their ex-spouse and drive-up legal costs.

DISCOVERY - TO GIVE OR NOT TO GIVE

The discovery process is often used to frustrate the legal process. Discovery can delay and disrespect the other party or overwhelm and intimidate them. In either case, the real purpose of discovery, to gather facts, is manipulated for the greater purpose of abusing the opposition.

Delaying responses is a typical maneuver in high-conflict divorces. Court rules require a party to respond to a discovery request within a certain amount of time. By delaying or failing to respond, your ex-spouse retains control of the process and costs you money in attorney's fees.

Suppose your ex-spouse owns their own business. You know many of their business transactions are conducted in cash, but your income tax returns do not reflect that. Instead, what is portrayed is an income grossly less than what you and your husband spent every year. You deduce that your ex-spouse must have another secret bank account, so you send discovery requesting that they produce statements from all their bank and investment accounts. Pursuant to the court rules, your ex-spouse has a limited time to respond. Assume they have 28 days. You eagerly wait out the month and on the 29th day you call your attorney, only to learn that your ex-spouse has not answered. Your attorney calls and politely agrees to the request for a delay as a professional courtesy. Perhaps two more weeks are "needed." At the end of two weeks, another call is made and another request for delay is granted, this time for five days. Your attorney assures you this is the last delay they will agree to. At the end of the two weeks, you receive ... nothing. Or perhaps you receive a very partial, uninformative response. In either case, you have now endured nearly two months without receiving any substantive information.

At a minimal rate of at least $100 per hour, your attorney drafts a **motion to compel** (asking the court to *require* your ex-spouse to respond to your discovery request), a **brief in support** (explaining the legal reasons why you are entitled to the information you seek), and other necessary documents such as a **proposed order**. The hearing is scheduled for next week. In the interim, you learn through your children that your ex-spouse went to Las Vegas on vacation. You mention it to your attorney, who promises to bring it to the court's attention, but they never have the chance. Instead, at the hearing, the judge asks your ex-spouse's attorney what the problem is. They calmly explain to the judge that *you* have all the records, there is nothing else except perhaps an old, closed-out account from five years ago, and that their client just found the bank statements from that account and will have them by next week. The court orders them to do so. You nudge your attorney because your ex-spouse did not pay the mortgage last week and went to Vegas instead, and you are certain there is a secret account because they practically admitted it when you called them about the mortgage. Before the judge can respond, your ex-spouse's attorney produces the mortgage check. The judge says, "I don't want to hear about any secret account," and the hearing is over. You have now spent thousands of dollars on attorney's fees and wasted weeks of time, and all you have to show for it is the mortgage check you were entitled to anyway.

Filing the motion to compel only benefited the attorneys. They make money pursuing whatever legal recourse you ask for. Although angry during the divorce proceedings, many people come to recognize that this type of legal maneuvering depletes the collective marital coffers, so they stop the competitiveness. In high-conflict cases, however, the personality-disordered spouse prefers sacrificing anything and everything for the thrill of winning. They will file that **motion to compel**. Should you pursue such a motion resulting in the circumstances described above, you have not only wasted time and money, but you have allowed your ex-spouse to "win" by controlling you. By filing the motion to compel, you become engaged in their conflict, demonstrating to them that they can still manipulate you. As long as you are willing to fight to prove your truths – that they are hiding money – you remain a willing participant in the conflict. Additionally, you have reinforced that you remain dependent on them for support, such as the mortgage. They remain in their position of power. A personality-disordered person who needs the "win" as much as they need air to breathe, thrives on this dynamic.

One way to avoid getting caught in this trap is to adjust the power balance. *You* use discovery as leverage. If you know your ex-spouse's clients, for example, subpoena them. Allan's ex-wife continually bragged she was a partner in her new husband's business. Allan, who had recently been awarded more time with his children, wanted to modify the child support he had been paying. Now that the kids were with their mom less and with him more, he felt he should pay less. His ex-wife, of course, was angry and refused to provide copies of her income tax returns. Allan circumvented her by sending subpoenas to third parties. Posted online was his ex-wife's new husband's client list. Subpoenas were sent to all the clients asking for invoices and receipts. Of course, this angered the new husband as he did not want his customers harassed by his wife's ex-husband, and the child support matter was quickly resolved. Similarly, if you subpoena all your ex-spouse's customers, you may cause them sufficient embarrassment that he will capitulate.

By circumventing your ex-spouse, either by acquiring copies of relevant documents on your own or from third parties, you undermine your ex-spouse's ability to use the discovery process to control and frustrate you. You also spend less money having your attorney issue subpoenas rather than preparing for and appearing in court. By allowing your ex-spouse to "cheat" on their discovery answers, you are letting them know they are not "getting to you." Besides, you can play the same game.

While the court rules require you to answer all questions fully, truth remains a malleable reality. All attorneys will tell you to answer discovery requests as minimally as possible. That is, do not volunteer more than is requested. But there are "minimums" and there are "minimums." If, for example, you are asked if you regularly drink alcohol, you can answer "yes" without elaborating. But if you are asked how much alcohol you drink in a week, you can choose how to answer. Assuming you do not consume the same number of drinks each week, you can respond with the maximum per week, the minimum per week, or the average. Why not answer based on the week you only had one drink? It is true, and how will your ex-spouse prove otherwise without hiring a private detective to follow you? This "truth" – that you only have one drink a week ~ remains the "truth" of your case unless it can be disproven. Your goal is to make proving this allegation so difficult that the issue is dropped.

Do not be the victim in the discovery process. You, too, can use it as a tool to even the playing field. Understand from the outset that you will not collect all the information you want, which is why you should copy all financial and legal documents when you still have access to them. Do not allow yourself to be dependent on your ex-spouse for information.

A WORD OF CAUTION

If the couple is amicable, they may exchange information without the need for discovery. But in high-conflict cases, the anger generates new anger and people become stubborn. They do not want to give up anything, on principle, and that includes not only bank records but an hour of time with the children. At some point, the divorce will be finalized and after a few years most people move on. But in high-conflict cases, entry into the legal process is not a means to the end: divorce. It is an education, enlightening one or both spouses of another tool for achieving goals: ongoing engagement. For high-conflict couples, the divorce is not an ending but simply another field for the couple to play on. It differs only in that the couple live apart. But unless one person changes the rules of the game, the control and abuse continue, and **motions** are an effective tool. Thus, the more frequently they are filed with the court and hearings are held, the more opportunity the personality-disordered ex-spouse has to learn how the system works and how to use it to their advantage. And because courts retain jurisdiction over a divorcing couple until the youngest child turns 18, parents in high-conflict cases may remain engaged in combat for a long time.

CHAPTER SIX:

The term "best interests of the child" was first coined in 1925 by the Supreme Court of New York. Before then, men were usually awarded custody of their minor children because children were seen as property and men had the financial ability to support them. In a custody dispute between father and mother, the New York judge challenged that precedent by declaring that he, the judge, should function as a "parents patriae" and do what is best for the interest of the child.[8] He would put himself in the position of a "wise, affectionate, and careful parent" and make the appropriate custody determination. Thus, the judge became the *uber-parent* who knew what was best for your children. As no-fault divorce spread across the country, judges began withdrawing from governing parental behavior. They no longer considered which parent was morally superior when granting a divorce and dividing assets. Instead, judges began deferring to the parents to decide custody if they could agree. The concept of determining custody based on the "best interests of the child" proliferated, although what that meant varied widely from state to state.

To promote consistency, the National Conference of Commissioners on Uniform State Laws adopted the Uniform

---

8 *Finlay v. Finlay*, 240 N.Y. 429, 148 N.E. 624 (N.Y. 1925).

Act in 1970. This act stated that the court shall determine custody in accordance with the best interest of the child, and that the court shall consider all relevant factors including:

- ❖ The parents' and child's wish for custody arrangements.
- ❖ The relationship of the child with parents, siblings, and others.
- ❖ The child's adjustment in the home, school, and community.
- ❖ The mental and physical health of all people involved.

This standard has since been adopted and elaborated upon by most states. Some states, like Michigan, have specific guidelines the court must consider. In Michigan, the law requires the judge to consider factors such as the moral fitness of the parties, the love and affection between the parties involved and the child, and the capacity of each party to give the child love, affection, and guidance. In Washington, a judge must consider a parenting plan that "best maintains a child's emotional growth, health and stability, and physical care." And in Missouri, one factor the court is required to consider is the "interaction and interrelationship of the child with parents, siblings and any other person who may significantly affect the child's best interests."

As women entered the workforce, courts began departing from the widely held belief that children needed their mothers more than their fathers. The trend began to move towards shared parental responsibility. The American Law Institute, a national non-profit group of lawyers and legal scholars who make recommendations about various areas of the law, recommended in 2004 that if parents cannot agree on custody, custodial responsibilities should be allocated based upon parents' past care-taking roles:

Unless otherwise resolved by agreement ... the court should

allocate custodial responsibility so that the proportion of custodial time the child spends with each parent approximates the proportion of time each parent spent performing care-taking functions for the child prior to the parents' separation...[9]

Not all states follow this guideline, and despite efforts to be gender-neutral, studies show that women are still primarily granted custody. Additionally, these guidelines have been criticized for failing to consider the quality of the parent-child attachment and for being unfair to working parents.

A WORD ABOUT CUSTODY

Most states distinguish between custody and parenting time. Often, they employ different terminology, but the fundamental concepts are consistent. Custody is often divided into **legal custody** and **physical custody**. When parents have legal custody, they have the right to make major decisions about their children. These decisions include issues about education, religious upbringing, and major medical matters. It is common for parents to share legal custody. Most courts allow parents to retain the right to make major decisions about their children's upbringing.

A parent who does not share legal custody with their children's other parent is said to have **sole legal custody**. In that case, the other parent has no right to make any decisions about the children,

---

9 Willemsen, E., Andrews, R, Karlin, B. & Willemsen, M. (2005). The ethics of the child custody process: are the American Law Institute's guidelines the answer? *Child & Adolescent Social Work Journal*. 22:2.

although they may still have visitation. It is difficult to get **sole legal custody** of your children. The prevailing philosophy is that a child is entitled to have a relationship with both parents. That your ex-spouse has a mental health issue or is emotionally abusive, or even physically abusive to you, will not dissuade the judge. In essence, your relationship with your ex-spouse is treated as a separate issue to your children's relationship with their other parent. You may believe your ex is evil and an awful parent, but your children have a legal right to a relationship with that parent and the court will do its best to preserve that right.

Physical custody is less likely to be shared. Some jurisdictions still give preference to the mother; others are more inclined to give joint or shared physical custody unless there is a significant reason not to. A parent who does not have sole or primary physical custody of their children still has rights to **parenting time**, formerly termed **visitation**. The children will spend weekends, holidays, midweek overnights, and vacations with that parent. When the children are with that parent, they participate in ordinary routines such as shopping, chores, homework, and spending other unstructured time together. The parent retains the right to make day-to-day decisions about the children's well-being when they are with them. In some states, this is called **joint physical custody**. In others it is not. Notably, in some states parenting time can amount to fifty percent or more and still not be labeled **joint physical custody**.

Some attorneys may advise you that having physical custody is unnecessary, especially if your children live with you fifty percent of the time. But that is not entirely true, especially in high-conflict cases. For one thing, some states still allow parents with physical custody to move with the children far from the other parent. Second, the parent without physical custody often loses decision-making power. The parent with physical custody may decide which primary physician the children will see, where they will play baseball, and which school they attend. They hold the passport, requiring the other parent to ask if they want to vacation with the children. They become the gatekeeper.

If there is a dispute, judges often resolve the matter based on who has physical custody, even if the law in that state requires a different inquiry. Dan's ex-wife agreed that their young children would remain in their current elementary school even though she moved out of the district. When their oldest son graduated and was ready to move on to middle school with his friends, she switched him to a school in her district. Dan believed this was the wrong decision because the boy had already experienced so much change in his young life. He was having difficulty socializing and Dan believed it was important for him to remain with his peer group. Because they could not agree, the matter was brought before the judge who decided that the child would move to the mother's school district simply because she had physical custody. This decision was made despite Michigan case law, which required the judge to hold a **best interest of the child hearing** when parents disagree about a child's school.

Parents who are not awarded physical custody often resent the other parent for their self-appointed "gatekeeper" role. Rather than fight, some parents make the best of it, preferring to spend their limited parenting time with their children going to a waterpark rather than supervising homework. These "Disneyland" parents have a bad reputation, but sometimes it is the other parent that created the situation. Unfortunately, while these Disneyland Parents may enjoy time with their children rather than *really* parenting them, studies show that their relationships with their children deteriorate, and parenting time often diminishes over time.

There is value to one parent having sole physical custody. Children living in one house benefit from the predictability and stability of that living arrangement. Routines can be maintained, and children do not have to bounce between two households, keeping track of things like homework and sports equipment. They do not need two of everything. Their lives are less hectic and more controlled.

Still, many parents like the idea of sharing physical custody. They believe it is fair and that it helps children maintain an ongoing relationship with both parents. But judges are still less inclined to award this type of custody if there is too much hostility between the parents. When parents share physical custody, they must live geographically close and have regular, frequent contact. They must be able to communicate, cooperate, and negotiate about everyday activities. In high-conflict cases, daily contact presents daily opportunities for abuse. Studies have found that parents who share parenting were fifty percent more likely to have conflicts over child-related issues than families where the children lived with one parent, simply because there was more interaction. And ongoing conflict is *known* to be detrimental to children's post-divorce adjustment. Joint physical custody is not always recommended in high-conflict cases then, as it keeps the door open between the parents.

GETTING CUSTODY

When you were married, you had unlimited access to your children. Now you have a judge – a stranger – deciding when you can and cannot see your children. This can be terrifying, especially if that judge is exposed to the countless lies being told about you. While judges do not often want to hear the "mud," they are cynical enough to recognize they do not always hear the truth either. Many courts require parents to undergo an evaluation to help them establish a custodial arrangement that is in the best interests of the children.

Mental health professionals usually conduct these evaluations. Their assignment is to assess the developmental needs of the children and each parent's ability to meet those needs. They then make recommendations, which have considerable influence on the judge. Most perform their job by interviewing the parents and children and observing their interactions with one another.

There are problems with this approach. Studies confirm that disputed custody cases can take be up to three times longer than undisputed divorces. The cost of the divorce is also greater, as parents must pay more in attorney fees, childcare costs, and sometimes therapy. They must also take more time off from work.

Furthermore, once again, an evaluation examines only a snapshot in time and fails to reflect the depth and breadth of the parent-child relationship. Aware of being observed, parents do their best to appear attentive to their children, but that does not expose whether the parent's attentiveness is genuine and sustainable, or if it is merely a performance. Aware of parent's propensity to perform, evaluators are cynical. So cynical, in fact, they sometimes discredit what is right before their eyes. Paul, a teenager with a genius IQ, was invited to speak to an evaluator, a court-appointed counselor. Paul agreed because he had a lot to say. But at the end of their conversation, the evaluator rejected everything Paul reported and accused his parent of coaching him, all because they thought his vocabulary was too advanced. The evaluator did not take the time to understand who Paul was before "evaluating" his narrative.

Critics challenge the professionalism of evaluators, noting that their methods lack scientific practices and empirical data. They suggest that evaluators fail to adhere to prescribed standards and that their recommendations to the judge can be biased and misleading. Nonetheless, because you are in a high conflict divorce you are likely to be evaluated sometime during the proceedings. Prepare yourself before the meeting. Do your best to obliterate from your mind all negative thoughts about your ex-spouse. Most evaluators are looking for two things: (1) your relationship with your children, and (2) whether you will foster or hinder your children's relationship with their other parent. Like all court personnel, they are not interested in that other parent's faults. If they ask what led to the break-up of the marriage, be vague. Say something such as, "It just didn't work out" or "We grew apart." Unless you have police reports documenting physical abuse, it will be their word against yours.

Your focus must be on your children and what is in their best interests. Use words like stability and consistency. But do not sound too rigid either. Suggest that you have been struggling to find a balance between ensuring your children have a good relationship with their other parent and continuing to give them opportunities to participate in activities that are essential for their development. If the evaluator challenges the proposed parenting plan you submitted, admit that you are new at this and still learning.

You must appear to be sincere. Before your meeting, imagine that "ideal divorce" where you and your former spouse remain friends and continue parenting together despite living in separate households. Keep that image in your mind throughout the meeting.

Any negative information about your ex-spouse that you believe should be shared with the evaluator should be transmitted through your attorney. Use them as your messenger. List all your evidence and then prioritize the most significant and damaging. Is it *that* important that your ex-spouse always returns the children late? Or is it more important that they allow your 7-year-old daughter to ride her bicycle without a helmet? You and your attorney should then select the top five to seven issues after which they will write a letter to the evaluator explaining your concerns. Provide specifics such as dates and times. This is especially important if you are alleging a pattern of negligent parenting. By having your attorney serve as your mouth-piece, you reduce the risk of the evaluator perceiving *you* as uncooperative or spiteful. They may still suspect that, but your attorney adds credibility to your complaints.

In the end, do not worry too much about the evaluator's recommendation. Neither of you will get exactly what you want. They will find some middle ground. But if they believe that you are acting in your children's best interests, they are more likely to favor you. Know also that their recommendation to the judge may never be read. Only about five percent of divorces go to trial. Your case, like most, is likely to be resolved at mediation.

MEDIATION:
NEGOTIATING FROM A POSITION OF POWER

Mediation involves a neutral, trained mediator who work with both parties (and attorneys if the parties wish) to discuss and resolve the issues. When the issues are resolved, the mediator drafts an agreement that you and your ex-spouse sign. This agreement becomes incorporated into a court order as part of your final judgment of divorce.

Mediation may occur any time before the trial. In some jurisdictions, mediation occurs early on, in recognition that the longer the process takes the more likely the couple's anger will become deeply entrenched. Resolution becomes more difficult. In other jurisdictions, mediation occurs closer to the trial date, after most of the discovery has been completed. This approach is based on the belief that divorce, like other civil actions, can only be resolved after the parties have all the necessary data. Some jurisdictions mandate mediation. In others, the judge has the discretion to order it.

For the average divorcing couple, mediation is an excellent tool. Mediation allows them to retain control over the outcome. Studies demonstrate that couples who mediate are more likely to abide by the agreements they reach. Mediation is far less costly than trial, and it focuses on problem solving rather than on personal attacks, thereby enabling the parties to co-parent after the divorce. But among high-conflict divorces, mediation's effectiveness is questionable. That is because many trained mediators are still unable to recognize abuse. The power imbalance that often exists in high-conflict marriages continues during the initial stages of the divorce. Abuse can be subtle.

Your former spouse will not openly threaten you. Rather, they will use body language, eye contact, or reference to past, private events as a means of reminding you that they are in control. The mediator does not recognize these nonverbal communications. Nor are your efforts to protect yourself and your children always recognized. If you refuse to agree to a proposal that seems "fair" on the surface, but you know is not, you may be perceived as being stubborn and inflexible. Unfortunately, studies have found that even when you confess the abuse you have experienced, mediators and lawyers do not always acknowledge your suffering. You may even be pressured by both the mediator and your attorney to accept a settlement.

It is important that the abused party does not embark on mediation until after establishing some safety protocols. Rather than sit in the same room with an abusive ex-spouse, demand that the mediator engage in **shuttle diplomacy.** That is, the parties sit in separate rooms and the mediator maneuvers back and forth between them. The mediator may resist this suggestion because it is less efficient, but it is safer because it allows the abused party time to think, and it liberates them from the other parent's diatribes about how much they love their children or need more than fifty percent of the marital property. You may also insist that you meet on different days. In either case, when the mediator presents an offer to you, it will not be laden with your former spouse's emotional pleas but will focus on the relevant issues. Your mediator is not likely to walk into your room, for example, and say, "Your spouse is so upset about how you never drive the kids to school." Rather, the mediator will say, "Your spouse wants you to return the kids at night and not in the morning on school days." You can choose to ask why, or you can simply respond to the bare proposal. A good mediator might neutrally question your reasons for your proposal, but a good mediator will also focus on the drop-off time (night or day) and not spend too much time discussing the veracity of the claim. If you were all in the same room, however, the conversation is more likely to veer off onto the tardiness issue and less likely to focus on resolution.

Mediation is a negotiation. That means you do not give up anything without getting something in return. Never propose everything you would be willing to agree to at the outset because then you have no room to negotiate. Always ask for more than you want, knowing you will have to give up some of your claims. If you want full custody, for example, offer your ex-spouse the "state's minimum:"[10] that is: every other weekend and one midweek visit. The *real* negotiation begins with the time. The midweek parenting time can be from after school on Wednesday to return to school on Thursday, or it can be only for dinner from 5-8 p.m. – or something in between. The same is true of the weekend parenting time. Weekend parenting time can begin Friday after school or Saturday morning at 10 a.m., and it can end on Monday return to school or on Sunday at 5 p.m. There are multiple options, and they will all affect the quality of your life and your children's. For example, if you believe your ex-spouse will not supervise your children's homework, you may want them returned to you earlier on Sunday. If your ex-spouse wants the children with them for Sunday night dinner, ask for something *you* want in exchange, such a later pick-up time on Wednesday. The take-home point is that anything you

---

10 A term used by one of my clients, which I adopted.

propose must have open edges that you can shrink in exchange for the things that are important to you.

Recognize that your ex-spouse is likely taking the same approach so do not be disheartened when they present a plan that is entirely favorable to them. But you can use the information to learn what your ex-spouse values, and what they are willing to give up. Pay attention. Bill and Meghan had accumulated a lot of debt. Bill earned a good salary but Meghan, a stay-at-home mom with two small children, had little earning potential and was terrified of having to pay off such a huge sum. During negotiation, Bill had derisively said to me that "debt is a tool." From that I understood he was not afraid of the debt. In the settlement they reached, Bill assumed *all* their debt and Meghan walked away debt-free in exchange for the house. While she loved her house, she would have had to sell it eventually because she could not afford to maintain it. Meghan's win-win was that she gave up something she did not have (the house) in exchange for something she did not want.

In another mediation, I represented a man who was breaking up with his business partners. My client wanted his partners to buy him out of the partnership. The only asset was a large piece of undeveloped property, and the issue was the price. The partners, of course, were low-balling the price so they would not have to pay him as much for his share, and he believed the price was much higher. This man's real goal was to own the property. Ultimately, he agreed to their price on the condition that if he secured additional financing within six months, they would agree to sell him *their* shares at the lower price. They agreed, believing he would never secure the financing. He did and, in the end, he acquired the entire parcel of land, which had been his ultimate goal. It is critical to listen to what the other party wants and what they are willing to give up.

Do not be afraid of saying "no" and threatening to take your chances at trial. It is a valid threat and even your personality-disordered spouse recognizes the costs and risks. The threat can be powerful leverage, bringing your ex-spouse to the negotiating table. Controlling people use it a lot. "If you don't agree, I'm going to take you to court and ask for *everything*" is a common threat in high-conflict divorces. Instead of being a victim to that, throw it right back. "If you don't agree, *I'm* going to go to court and ask for *everything*." Lindsey's husband was an attorney. She wanted to mediate their divorce and he agreed to the process, but they never resolved the issues. After 20 hours of ineffective mediation, Lindsey retained me. The first thing we did was file a motion in court to dispel her husband's belief that she was afraid of litigation. Lindsey's husband had understood her trepidation of trial and was "mediating" for the sole purpose of wearing her down. He was playing "chicken," waiting for her to "blink," at which time he believed she would give up everything she had been asking for. Lindsey's mistake was letting him know that she was afraid of court. For him, it was simply a waiting game. Once Lindsey dispelled him of his belief that she would not fight, he understood that he had to negotiate in good faith. They resolved their issues much faster once she could legitimately threaten trial as an acceptable means of resolving their issues. Try holding out on critical issues until the other party "blinks" first.

Be willing to "up the ante" also. Negotiations are flexible and until you sign on the dotted line, you are free to change your mind. Kristen and her ex-husband had agreed on custody and parenting time, but before the deal was signed, she developed *buyer's remorse*. She did not like the terms she had agreed to and wanted to change them. Her ex-husband responded by "upping the ante." That is, in the next negotiation he asked for even more parenting time. He knew he would accept the original plan. He knew his wife would agree to the original plan, or something similar, because she had already done so. But by scaring her into believing that he would seek even more, Kristen's ex-husband convinced her to accept the original agreement.

Negotiation is a chess game. You will not get everything you want. You will get less than you ask for. So, ask for more than you can agree to, *knowing ahead of time what you are willing to give up.* By knowing this, you create a dynamic where your opponent is collaborating with you rather than against you. After much "persuasion" to get you to agree to give up something you already planned on relinquishing, your opponent feels they won something; and you can exact a price for whatever it is you "gave up." Zoe's son wanted to attend sleepover camp with his friends, but the boy's father argued that he loved his son and wanted the son to spend the time with him. Zoe knew that her ex-husband worked long hours and left their son in daycare, but after years of conflict she learned that this argument carried no weight with judges and mediators. The father had a legal right to time with his son, even if that time was spent with the boy languishing in daycare. Zoe also knew the father wanted their son to have a passport. Although she had concerns about him taking their son out of the country, Zoe was advised that she would lose that issue. So, Zoe embarked on mediation knowing she would give in on the passport issue in exchange for the father's agreement that their son be allowed to attend camp. The father agreed. The mediator felt successful. And Zoe and her son got what they wanted without losing anything. By knowing ahead of time what she was willing to give up, Zoe controlled the dialogue.

Do not let your ex-spouse pressure you into agreeing to something prematurely. If the offer is only on the table for a brief amount of time, do not take it. You need time to think it through and understand all the ramifications of the deal. You need time to examine the proposal for hidden pitfalls. You are entitled to that and, again, there is nothing in a divorce case that should require instant answers. If your former spouse claims they have an offer to buy their boat, for example, and you *must* agree to sell it immediately, be skeptical. That third party who is "demanding" an immediate answer from your ex-spouse (who is, in turn, "demanding" an immediate answer from you), is not your problem. More likely than not, your ex-spouse has been negligent in responding to that third party, who is now frustrated and making threats. Your ex-spouse's problems are not your problems. You no longer need to rescue them. But what you do need is to be certain that the deal you strike is best for you.

Nor should you respond to an "all or nothing" deal. If that is the offer, then you are better off walking away. Again, pressure to respond immediately without giving you time to think through the ramifications of the proposal is a control tactic. If your ex-spouse were seriously interested in resolving issues, they would allow you time to think things through and provide counteroffers or identify problems so that the ultimate agreement makes sense for both of you. All or nothing deals, or take it or leave it deals, are one-sided and should be rejected.

In sum, before entering a negotiation:

- ❖ Always ask for more than you want, knowing that you will get less, and knowing that your ex-spouse is doing the same.
- ❖ Know what you want and what you are willing to give up. Periodically re-examine what is important to you and do not remain trapped in old needs or wants that no longer make sense.
- ❖ Be prepared to say, "I need to think about this. Let me take it home and study it and I will get back to you."
- ❖ Always know that you can say, "We can always go to court and let the judge decide."

Keep notes of what your ex-spouse is willing to give up. This will give you insight into their values, needs, and wants. It will also help you posture if there is a second round of mediation. If your ex-spouse is willing to give up the house during the first round of negotiations, for example, they are likely to be willing to give it up again.

LITIGATION

Litigation is challenging for many reasons. It is costly, time-consuming, stressful and, most disturbing, it is an arena where a stranger decides your future. The results can be unpredictable and the process uncomfortable at best.

The prevailing **best-interests-of-the-child** standard offers little guidance to judges and remains vague. When considering what arrangements are in the best interests of the child, some courts have guidelines, and some do not. Some guidelines are listed in a statute, and some have been developed by case law. Whatever factors the guidelines require a judge to consider, family court is a court of **equity** and that means the judge has discretion to do what they believe is **just.** Justice is not always fair, and justice is not always just. The judge starts off with a belief that the child has a right to a relationship with both parents. While some judges still have a bias towards mothers, many judges are swayed by the father who declares love for his offspring and professes a powerful desire to parent. If the father wants to spend time with his children, then you, the mother, do not make a good impression trying to impede that relationship.

Furthermore, the system promotes hostile litigation, which is polarizing. The adversarial nature of the court system aggravates parents' conflicts by pitting them against each other. To "win" custody, parties must expose the faults and weaknesses of the other parent. Some people, especially those that are personality disordered and have a sense of entitlement, believe that the ends justify the means. Their fear of losing control – over you, the children, and their property – amplifies that behavior. Or they are pursuing custody simply to intimidate, hurt, and manipulate you. Regardless, they will deliberately provoke their adversary, you, their former spouse. And they will be righteously indignant if you expose their faults (which they deny exist). Again, their behavior may not be overt. Instead, they will display their **Public Persona**, that warm and charming person you dated and married. The inside or *real personality* will be hidden. Your effort to show the court the "real" person, the one you lived with, is an uphill battle. In this "winner takes all" scenario, there is no path to recovery.

But what you believe is horrible parenting or horrible behavior may not be awful enough to justify losing rights. In fact, you give credence to the other parent's argument that you are trying to alienate them from their children if you relentlessly pursue your cause. Similarly, if a mother wants to spend time with her children and the father is trying too hard to wrestle custody from her, then he appears to be a bully. Your **Courtroom Persona** must walk a fine line between pursuing your agenda of maximizing your own custody award, while simultaneously appearing as if you are not trying to undermine your children's other parent. You must talk in terms of the *best interests of the child.*

Despite its ambiguity, our culture does have some consensus about what is right for children. For example, it is understood that a nursing mother should have custody of the infant so that she can continue to nurse. It is also understood that a teenager will want more flexibility in a plan so that they can spend time with friends or at extracurricular activities. Parents who fail to recognize these "truths" and who argue they "love their children and want to spend as much time as possible with them," can be "defeated" by pointing out that this parent is not considering a plan that is in the child's best interests. Be calm and rationale when making this argument. Leave it to your friends to embellish in their testimony about what an ogre your ex-spouse really is. By painting this broad picture, by showing you are thinking of the children's needs, you have a better chance of the judge accepting the parenting plan you propose rather than your ex-spouse's.

If you can explain to the judge why it is in your children's best interests to live with you and visit their other parent every other weekend, then you should do so. How do you do that? Talk about all the parenting you do, how involved you are in the children's lives, how you coach their teams, etc. You should also talk about how little parenting the other parent does but try to limit your argument to their actions (or lack thereof) and not their character. Remember that calendar you kept which tracked when your ex-spouse missed parenting time or was late getting the children? Now is the time to produce it. Let the facts speak for themselves.

Talk about the importance of schedules and structure. Speak of the children's need for time to do homework and how you work with them every night. Speak of religious school and religious services; speak of the importance of preserving the children's ties to their community, friends, and family. Mention that the schedule proposed by the other parent is disruptive and not in the children's best interests. Talk about how much you love your children and how much they love you. Talk about all the things you do together: how little Bobbie loves the special pancakes you make for him on Sunday mornings with the chocolate chip happy face, or how Suzie loves when you brush out her hair after her bath and you sing special songs together. Create an image of you and your kids bonding, and that will go a long way towards convincing the court that you are the primary parent.

Establish your record as an active and involved parent. Maintain records demonstrating how you have complied with every **temporary order**. Provide proof of your involved parenting. Include in your pleadings, **affidavits** from teachers and coaches that verify you participate in your child's life. Any email written favorably about you and your child should be produced. Include pictures of you and your child at hockey practice or on the roller coaster at the amusement park. Your own supporting affidavit should include an anecdote about the special relationship you have with your children as well as detailed information about what you do as a parent. If you are the parent who helps with the homework, say so. If you are the parent that arranges play dates or summer camp, say so. Do not be shy. Now is the time to show the court that you are the primary parent.

Assume your ex-spouse will lie. Do not get into a "he-said-she-said" debate. Instead, try exposing their lies by producing their interrogatories. If they wrote something under oath that differs from what they said in court, you will have solid proof of their dishonesty. If not, the affidavits of friends will help. When you ask them to write on your behalf, ask them to include a brief negative statement about your ex-spouse. As always, they should not be too demonizing because, like you, they risk being dismissed as biased and unreliable. Also, they may feel uncomfortable. Ask each friend, instead, to mention one thing. Your best friend, for example, might describe how they came over late at night with medicine for your sick child because your ex-spouse was not at home. Your neighbor might write about the time they heard your ex-spouse shouting at you. Each little detail adds to the picture you are painting.

Your objective is to get custody of your children. Your emotions are high. You are probably feeling depressed, anxious, helpless, and desperate. But this is the crucial time to wear your **Courtroom Persona**. Maintain the image that you are calm, measured, reasonable, and dependable. The more reasonable you appear to be, the more likely the judge will gravitate towards you. You cannot count on "breaking your ex-spouse" so they expose their real self. They have spent a lifetime perfecting their **Public Persona**. As uncomfortable as this may feel, as much as you want the judge to see that *you* are the better parent and the victim, as much as you want them to validate your truths, the risk is too great. Remember that it is more difficult for judges to choose between two people arguing about what they want, than to choose between one parent who claims to love their children and the other parent who is badmouthing the first. You will get more of what you want by making the judge chose between two good parents, rather than one good and one bad. If you fail to protect your image and are branded as the bad parent, you *will* lose more than you will gain.

THE PARENTING PLAN

Even if you get custody, your ex-spouse will have parenting time with the children. Unless your ex-spouse has molested a child, is proven likely to kidnap the children, or is using illegal drugs or drinking excessively while caring for the children, they will not be denied visitation. A judge may restrict it, however, requiring that visitation be supervised. Regardless, a parenting plan will have to be developed. Ninety-five percent of the time, this will happen in mediation.

Ideally, the parenting plan should be child-centered, reflecting each child's age-appropriate needs as well as their individual needs. For infants and toddlers (birth to two years), for example, being apart from their primary parent, even for a few hours and even with someone familiar, can be stressful. A primary parent is usually the stay-at-home parent, or the parent who is primarily responsible for feeding, dressing, changing, and nurturing the child.

Parents who no longer live with their young children must be patient, giving them time to become reacquainted with each visit. Frequent contact will help, but the schedule should allow for the children's routines to remain intact. Routines such as mealtimes, bedtimes, and early morning rituals reinforce the children's feelings of comfort and security. Make certain the baby's or toddler's "lovies" (favorite toy or blanket) transfer with the child.

Even young children can sense the feelings of an upset parent and can become upset, too. Children ages three to five often personalize any hostility they sense between their parents and interpret it as being their fault. This is because at that age they are "all about me." As with infants and toddlers, preschoolers need frequent, short visits with the parent who has moved away. A familiar routine helps re-establish feelings of security. Regular contact with both parents is recommended, with an understanding that if the schedule is disrupted, young children can become terribly upset.

School-age children (ages six to eleven) can tolerate more time away from each parent. Again, regular contact with both parents is recommended, but now the parenting plan should include flexibility to allow for extracurricular activities and social relationships. Because children at this age are learning to relate to the larger world, they are beginning to make independent decisions and seek help and comfort from non-family members. They are developing extracurricular obligations and social networks that expand beyond the home. For these reasons, parenting time schedules must be more flexible to allow for these new responsibilities.

Teenagers often challenge their parents, but a child experiencing a high-conflict divorce may choose to divorce themselves from one or both parents. For these young adults, it is important they remain in their current school where they have already developed a network of friends. Respecting that child's healthy social and extracurricular needs is critical.

Barry refused to allow his four-year-old son to keep his regularly scheduled Friday play date with his best friend. He claimed that since it was his parenting time, he had control over the boy's schedule. While technically this was correct, Barry was not thinking about his son. He was thinking about his ex-wife. She had arranged this play date when she was a stay-at-home-mom, and he was not going to participate in anything she had initiated. He did not care that this was a special time for his son. He made his decision based on his need to control his son's time and to show her she had lost all influence when their son was with him.

It is important, then, when presenting your plan, to include language respecting your children's developmental stages and personality. You are more likely to achieve success if you argue that your 3-year-old needs a 7 p.m. bedtime and therefore an 8 p.m. transfer is not in their best interests. While your ex-spouse may be arguing that they want more time with their children, you are focusing the court on that child's needs.

THE DEVIL IS IN THE DETAILS

In high-conflict cases, an ambiguous plan will create ongoing post-judgment litigation. The plan must be incredibly detailed, with nothing capable of multiple interpretations. It is difficult to predict the many ways a parent can interpret a plan to maximize their own parenting time while minimizing the other's. Heather's judgment of divorce required her ex-husband to contribute to child-care costs during working hours. Heather had a full-time job that paid enough to support her. At night, she often taught line-dancing at her local community center. Even though her ex-husband would have happily taken the kids, she left them with a babysitter and demanded he pay because she interpreted her nighttime activities as "working hours."

Emma interpreted her ex-husband's "week" of parenting time as less than seven days because the order used the words "at the beginning of parenting time" and *she* did not have "parenting time," she had "custodial time." And Madison tried prohibiting her ex-husband from attending their son's doctor appointment because it occurred on "her time." In fact, when he arrived at the doctor's office, Madison, and her new husband very publicly yelled at him to leave and threatened to call the police.

The ways a personality-disordered parent can distort the plain language of a parenting plan are endless. Jillian and her children lived several states away from her ex-husband. The parenting plan allowed him to visit once a month, arriving on Wednesday or Thursday and leaving on Sunday or Monday. Jillian's ex-husband refused to tell her what day and time he would arrive and when he would return the children. In this way, he held her hostage because she could not plan when to be home for her children. When Jillian agreed to this plan, she never anticipated her ex-husband would be so intentionally inconsiderate. But people are creative and self-serving. Endeavor to draft a plan that is extremely detailed and anticipates the many ways your ex-spouse might interpret it to favor himself or herself.

Divide your plan into categories. Consider different schedules for the school year and summer. Your plan should also account for holidays, vacations, and special occasions. When crafting a school plan, consider:

- ❖ When will the school schedule take affect? Will it begin the day before school starts, the weekend before, or a week before?
- ❖ During the school week, will there be visits and, if so, will they be overnight visits? How many? What time will the visits begin and end? Will pick-up and return be at school or at each parent's house?
- ❖ What if there is no school? Will return be to a parent's house and, if so, what time?
- ❖ When will weekend visits start and end? Will they begin after school on Friday at 5 p.m. or on Saturday at 10 a.m.? When will weekend visits end? Will they end on Sunday afternoon at 5 p.m., Sunday evening at 8 p.m., or return to school on Monday? What if there is no school on Monday?
- ❖ What if there is no school or a half-day of school on Friday? Will that change the other parent's parenting time?

Consider which school holidays will be included in the plan. Will the plan include alternating Martin Luther King, Memorial, and Labor Day holidays? Will the parent who had the children the prior weekend keep them on the Monday holiday or will Monday holidays be rotated independent from the weekend? If Monday holidays are independent of the prior weekend, what is the start and end time of the holiday?

What other holidays, such as Halloween, will your plan include? What time will those holidays begin and end? Will that change as the children grow older? When will Thanksgiving begin and end, on Wednesday after school or Thursday morning? Will it end on Thursday, Friday, or will the weekend be included as part of the holiday?

School vacations are challenging if the school calendar is not consistent year to year. Consider whether you will alternate the winter and spring break holidays or divide them in half. How will you and your ex-spouse divide Christmas and New Year's? What times will the holidays start and end, and will the pick-up and return be at school or at your house?

When you consider summer vacation, first ponder the number of weeks each parent will have. Deliberate whether the vacation weeks will be consecutive or divided so that no parent must endure two or four weeks without seeing the children. Which parent chooses their vacation first and when will the vacation weeks start and end? I know several people whose ex-spouses scheduled vacations to consume all the other parent's weekends, practically eliminating all summer weekend parenting for that parent. One solution is to limit summer weeklong vacations to one weekend that would be that parent's. In other words, the week you took with your children would start on your Friday and end on the following Friday, so that the other parent could have their regularly scheduled weekend. What if your children want to go to overnight summer camp? Will that occur on your week or on a regularly scheduled shared week?

It is challenging to prepare for every eventuality, and you cannot anticipate *every* way your ex-spouse will distort the plan's language to benefit themself. However, the more details you can secure, the less opportunity for abuse.

POTENTIAL PITFALLS

Will the other parent pick up the children at the start of their parenting time or will you drop the kids off?

Who will bring the kids back to your house, you, or the other parent?

Transportation and communication are two areas that create chronic conflict. If pick-up and drop-off is not at school, then exchanging at the house is most comfortable for the children. If you do not feel safe, include language that prevents the other parent from coming to the door or entering your house. Another option is to exchange the children at a neutral place. Some couples chose McDonald's or Starbucks.

Parents will want to communicate with their children when they are away. But some parents want to place limits on the other parent's contact. David's ex-wife denied her teenage children email accounts so that they could not communicate with their father. If your ex-spouse makes these types of demands and you suspect your judge will agree to them, be sure they apply to both of you. Do not allow the court to restrict only you.

Cell phones raise a plethora of issues. Who will pay for it? If you pay for your children's cell phone, be certain your ex-spouse knows that phone belongs to you. Do not allow them to take the phone away as a "punishment." If your ex-spouse pays for the child's cell phone, will there be restrictions? Heather bought her small children a limited cell phone to be used for emergencies only. She uploaded her telephone number and their stepfather's but refused to allow the children to call their father on this phone. She even lied to her children, telling them that the phone could only accept two telephone numbers. Heather's ex-husband felt impelled to purchase a second phone for the children, and they were forced to carry two telephones until Heather relented.

Religion is another realm that generates conflict. If a parent deviates from the religious practices the family followed when they were intact, the other parent might demand the children return to those prior religious practices. I know of parents who have sued one another for failing to feed the children kosher food. Your parenting plan should anticipate how you and your ex-spouse will raise the children if either of you plan to modify your religious practices. Include language that recognizes and respects each parent's right to practice religion in their own manner and raise the children in accordance with their individual practices. If your ex-spouse is reluctant to agree to such language, try assuring them that you have no immediate plans to change religion but want to protect both of your rights to become observant. Your objective is to secure your right to practice your religion at the outset so that your ex-spouse is prevented from using religion as an excuse for post-divorce litigation.

Travel plans should be considered. Will there be restrictions on traveling out of state or out of the country? Will parents be required to exchange travel itineraries with one another? If parents must exchange itineraries, when will the exchange occur? Jillian's ex-husband was required to provide her with a copy of the children's itinerary whenever they traveled out of state. He complied with the order but waited to give Jillian the itinerary at the time he picked up the children. This prevented her from planning ahead and making her own vacation plans while the children were out of state. While he complied with the court order, he did so in a way designed to harass his ex-wife.

Parents will be required to cooperate in acquiring the children's passports, but who will hold those documents? Will one parent have a right to deny the passports from the other and under what conditions? What notice will be required to exchange the passport from one parent to another? Dan's ex-wife wanted to keep the passports every time the kids were with her, but she had no job, no family, and had spoken about her dream of living "off the grid." Dan was fearful she would kidnap the children and resisted giving her the passports unless she had definite travel plans.

Another issue to consider is when are the children able to fly alone? Many parents in high-conflict cases try to prevent their ex-spouses from attending their children's extracurricular activities. Sarah's ex-husband tried forcing her to attend every other school field trip because he did not want to see her when he was there. Include in your parenting plan a statement that each parent has the right to attend all the children's activities. But know that even with this language, motivated parents will find a way to subvert the spirit of the plan. Maryanne refused to tell her ex-husband whether she planned to take the children to their school's ice cream social. He had been invited to another event but preferred attending the children's activity so he could spend a little time with them. Although Maryann's refusal to communicate did not violate the letter of the plan, she succeeded in retaining her control over her ex-husband.

To some, it may be trivial, but to others, trophies and schoolwork are prizes. Imagine you are the assistant coach of your son's Little League team. At the end of the season, trophies are distributed. But it is your ex-spouse's parenting time. Even though you worked all spring with your son and his team, your ex-spouse walks home with the trophy, which now lives at their house. Or imagine you spent weeks helping your daughter with her science project. You helped her research her idea, construct her model, conduct the experiment, and prepare an elaborate poster and Power Point presentation. But the open house falls on her other parent's time and, at the end of the evening, they collect the project and take it to their home.

Allen's ex-wife actually sued him to keep the children's homework. She argued that because she had physical custody of the kids, she had physical custody of the homework, too. Unfortunately, there is not much you can do legally, but know that your ex-spouse understands that by dominating your children's work product they are continuing to assert control over you. Otherwise, the two of you would have developed a system of sharing.

A WORD ABOUT FRIENDLY-PARENT LEGISLATION

A word of caution about "friendly parent" provisions, which have been enacted in over thirty states. These laws require judges to favor the parent perceived as most willing to foster a relationship between the children and the other parent. Based on the premise that maintaining close contact with both parents is in the children's best interests, any unwillingness by a parent to facilitate access to the other parent is punished. Some states require judges to consider a parent's "unfriendliness" or alienating behavior as a rationale for granting custody to the other parent. These laws are particularly dangerous in high-conflict and abuse cases.

Judges do not always recognize when abusers deliberately provoke their ex-spouse until they respond by attacking physically or verbally. Or perhaps they flee with the children. Because judges are unaware of or unwilling to examine the circumstances surrounding the "unfriendly" – abused – parent's actions, they often give custody to the abusive ex-spouse who presented themselves as a caring, devoted parent willing to communicate.

There is also a reluctance to consider a parent's abusive behavior as a reflection of their parenting. You know if your ex-spouse is emotionally abusing your children, but in "friendly-parent" states you are severely limited – if not helpless – to do anything about it without appearing as if *you* are the alienating parent.

Unless judges, mediators, and other legal professionals are aware of the subtle ways in which abuse can occur, reluctance to communicate or cooperate with your ex-spouse may be perceived as unwillingness to cooperative or "unfriendly." In your situation, "friendly parent" legislation may damage your chance at custody unless you are extremely diligent at maintaining your **Courtroom Persona**.

DEVIATING FROM THE PLAN

Once the plan is approved, you and your ex-spouse can always agree to deviate from it. If both of you agree to switch a weekend, for example, there is no reason for a court to get involved. Remember to record every agreement in a confirming email. While your private agreements with your ex-spouse are not enforceable in that they are not court-ordered, the judge will still consider your written agreement if a conflict erupts.

If the deviation establishes a new arrangement that is favorable to you and your children, then try to maintain it as long as possible. For example, if you and your ex-spouse agree that even though pick-up under the plan was from school, they will collect the children from your home after school ends, so the children can gather their belongings, confirm that agreement in writing and then try to maintain the new agreement as long as possible. If your ex-spouse then decides to renege on your agreement, not only will you have a writing confirming the agreement, but you will have consistency on your side. You are now positioned to argue in favor of a **modification** of the plan to accommodate the new arrangement because: (a) both parents agreed, (b) the arrangement meets your children's needs, (c) your children have become accustomed to the new arrangement and (d) it would be disruptive to change things yet again. All these arguments support your claim that the new arrangement is in your children's best interest. You might even go as far as to argue to the judge that by allowing your ex-spouse to renege they will become emboldened to further disrupt any agreements you have made. If you lose, the worst-case scenario is that you go back to the original plan and know that you can never agree to deviate from the plan again unless the agreement is codified in a court order.

MODIFYING THE PARENTING PLAN

Modification on the grounds that the parenting plan is not working, is an uphill battle. It is widely accepted that children need a stable home environment to thrive. Consistency is considered essential for childhood development, and it is strongly believed that children need a stable home life. The deeply rooted prevailing philosophy is that once a custody arrangement and parenting plan is in place, it should not be changed. This is such a strongly held belief that Michigan's 1970 Uniform Marriage and Divorce Act provided that modification of custody shall not occur unless there has been a "change of circumstances of the child or his custodian, and that the modification is necessary to serve the best interest of the child."

This doctrine is designed to assure continuity for the child. Most states have adopted a variation of this rule. Washington State, for example, requires a "substantial change of circumstances," and Michigan requires merely a "change of circumstances." Ordinary growth from a toddler to a teenager is not a change of circumstances. Remarriage or a significant change in a child's behavior or academic performance, do constitute a change of circumstances. In either case, the proposed change must be in the best interests of the child.

Modification is therefore a two-step process. First, the moving parent (the parent filing the **motion to modify** the parenting plan) must prove to the court that there has been a change of circumstances. *Then* there is a hearing to determine what the new custody arrangement or parenting plan will be. This gives your ex-spouse two opportunities to fight the proposed changes. They can argue there is no change of circumstances worthy of modifying the plan, and then they can argue against the changes you propose. Modifications are time consuming and costly.

In high-conflict divorces, constant re-litigation of parenting issues can give rise to modification. The most common post-judgment issues that are re-litigated are visitation and child support. The conflicts will be over small issues such as ambiguities in your parenting plan, and larger issues such as chronically unworkable schedules. Sometimes new issues arise. Ultimately, the same types of issues that could not be resolved without court intervention during the divorce continue to arise **post-judgment.** It is tempting to return to court because the years of conflict have intensified your mistrust, antagonism, and fear, which sometimes unreasonably prohibits you from relinquishing any control and fighting against what you perceive as an ongoing invasion of your rights. You feel that you need help to maintain control over your life and your children's lives. If there is too much post-judgment litigation however, a court may **sua sponte** (on the judge's own accord) order the custody and parenting plan to be modified. This may or may not work out in your favor and is one of the dangers of being a litigation **Frequent-Flyer.**

If you chose to legally modify your parenting plan yourself, it is imperative to prepare properly. Preserve all records that support your argument. Document when parenting time did or did not occur. Collect emails verifying this. Document the changes in your children's behavior, academic performance, or emotional state. Collect school and medical records. Secure affidavits from adult witnesses such as coaches and teachers. Use a calendar to record events as they occur. Include the names of people involved and the outcome. To modify a parenting plan, you must have sufficient evidence of both a **change in circumstances** and that your proposed plan is in your children's **best interests**.

Your first hurdle is to prove a change of circumstances. You *will* meet resistance, so anticipate what arguments your ex-spouse is likely to use to deny there has been a change of circumstances. Formulate responses. Then, when drafting your **motion** and **affidavit,** include those responses to their strongest arguments. Try to "head them off at the pass." When presenting your data to the court, make it as visually accessible as possible. Use a timeline or graph, numbers, or bullet-points, to highlight the various events justifying the change of circumstances. As always, arrive in court wearing your **Courtroom Persona**.

Once the judge agrees that the plan may be modified, they will grant you additional time to prepare your case proving that your proposed plan is in the best interests of your children. If mediation was moderately successful before, you may try mediating again. But do not offer it immediately. Allow your ex-spouse time to consider the cost and precariousness of another trial. Perhaps serve them with another set of interrogatories, or subpoena records that are exclusively in their possession. Use all your leverage, including information you have gained over the years, of what frightens them and what they are willing to give up. Your objective is to reduce their resistance by convincing them that you are determined to proceed. These initial efforts may save you the time and expense of a trial.

Do not request that your children, now older, testify. Many people ask when a child is old enough to make their own decisions about the parenting plan. The answer is 18. Some judges will meet with a child and consider that child's input, but you cannot initiate that meeting. Judges understand that even if a child is angry at or professes to hate a parent, that child is still conflicted. We are all hardwired to want our parents' love and approval. If you invite your child to testify, you may appear to be coaching the child, and you *never* want that. Judges do not want one parent coaching a child to choose. In sum, modifications of custody and parenting arrangements can be as costly and stressful as the initial divorce. Remember that court is only one tool, and you can make changes in different ways. Consider a long-term strategy. If your children are older, changes may occur naturally. Your ex-spouse may lose interest in the children if there is no battle to fight. Your teenagers may be busy with school, work and friends, and your ex-spouse may not want the hassles of constant re-scheduling. In these cases, time may accomplish what the court system could not. If the children are younger, you may find ways to "tweak" the plan so that it is more manageable. After six months or a year of these minor revisions, consider asking your ex-spouse to agree to a **consent order** codifying these changes. Be careful because you risk "waking the sleeping giant" and giving them new cause to fight you. But if you do end up in court, argue that these changes have become the "new normal" and it is important that your children's lives remain stable and consistent. If you chose not to formally change the plan, consider your extra time with your children a gift, and know that the possibility exists that you will revert to the original court order. It is something you have lived with before so it should not be too painful of a pill to swallow.

CHAPTER SEVEN:

I ssues surrounding child support often generate conflict. Many people are reluctant to pay child support because they believe the money is not used for the child. Jared's ex-wife had breast enhancement surgery immediately after their divorce. She also purchased expensive electronics. Yet she refused to support their children's extracurricular activities, claiming she had no money. While Jared continued paying support, inside he seethed because of his ex-wife's refusal to spend the money on their children.

Other **payor parents** (the parent owing the support) feel they are paying too much. They cannot afford the amount of support required of them, or they believe they are "double paying" because they spend money on their children when the children are with them. Perhaps they buy their children clothes because the **payee** (the parent receiving the support check) refuses to buy enough. Or perhaps the payee parent does not purchase the children's school supplies. At the same time, however, the payee parent may believe the amount is insufficient to support the children's "real" needs. Or they are resentful when they see their ex-spouse spending money on themself or their new family. Whatever the reason, the payment of child support can provide a constant source of tension among high-conflict divorced parents.

Many states have a definitive policy that child support may not be linked to custody and parenting time. If the payor fails to pay, the payee may not deny parenting time. The temptation is great, however. It is logical to think that if a parent refuses to support their children why should that parent enjoy time with them? Denying parenting time, however, is grounds for a contempt citation.

Surprisingly, some states do link child support with parenting time. In these states, the number of overnights children spend with the **payor** parent is inversely proportional to the amount of child support payments. Consequently, parents in these states sometimes demand more time with their children for the sole purpose of reducing their child support payments. Not surprisingly, this tactic engenders more conflict between the ex-spouses.

Base child support transfer payments are determined by calculating each parent's net income. Mandatory and voluntary deductions are considered when determining "income," including contributions to pension plans and retirement accounts, and payments to children from a prior marriage or relationship. Because this flexibility in calculating a parent's net income exists, establishing the initial base child support transfer figure can generate conflict. If the parents live in a state that links child support to the number of overnights a child spends with each parent, the conflict intensifies. This is an issue worth fighting.

A parent who wishes to "buy" their children is not acting in their best interests. Do your best to inform the court of your ex-spouse's tactics. Refuse to agree to a transfer payment so that the judge must decide the issue. If possible, file the motion to determine child support yourself so that you can explain to the judge that your ex-spouse is trying to amass parenting time for the sole purpose of reducing child support.

All states have an agency tasked with facilitating the transfer of child support payments. These agencies are also mandated to assist in child support modifications. Like many bureaucratic organizations, however, their inefficiencies often create tremendous frustration that exacerbates the conflict between ex-spouses. Modifications of child support, for example, are not usually retroactive. Thus, if a parent seeks to increase or decrease support, months may pass before a new support order is entered. During that time, one parent is paying more or receiving less than is appropriate. And when the new order is finally entered, a parent may feel they lost months of income. Even though this situation may benefit your ex-spouse and harm you, do your best to differentiate the sources of your frustration. Recognize that while your ex-spouse may be reaping the benefits of bureaucratic inefficiencies, they had no control. By misplacing your anger onto your ex-spouse, you risk prolonging or even enhancing the conflict and stress in your life. Unfortunately, there are other child support issues where you can legitimately blame your ex-spouse for causing you stress and costing you money.

HEALTH CARE EXPENSES: THERAPY, BRACES AND MORE

While many states require child support figures to include the payment of health care expenses, this does not usually include "elective" health care costs such as therapy and braces.

Whether or not children need therapy is an issue that generates tremendous conflict among divorcing and divorced parents. In high-conflict divorces, one parent often believes the children need therapy to assist them in coping with the break-up of their family, while the other parent does not. Some people do not see any benefit to therapy. Some parents are ashamed or fearful of what their children will say to the therapist. Some parents see the therapist as a tool of the other parent, who will be manipulated to testify against them. Whatever the reason, providing therapy to a child whose other parent rejects the idea, presents a significant challenge.

If parents share legal custody, one parent does not have the unilateral right to have a minor child treated by a therapist. The need for therapy is considered a joint legal decision, requiring both parents to agree. Knowing that, most therapists are reluctant to treat a child of divorced parents without both parents' consent. Therapists do not want to develop a relationship that might be severed by court order, and they certainly prefer not being hauled into court to testify.

If your ex-spouse refuses to agree to therapy for your minor child, you will need a court order. This is an issue I do not recommend giving up. You child needs the support during this tremendously stressful time in their life. Equally important is the lesson you teach your child; that you are willing to fight for them. By doing so, your child learns which parent really cares about their needs and which parent does not. You have not "denigrated" the other parent, but you have provided a clear contrast between the parent who fights to provide for your child's needs and the parent who fights against them. This one lesson will go a long way in helping your child cope because they will understand you are on their side.

Before filing a motion requesting therapy, send your ex-spouse a list of proposed therapists and ask them to research and select one.

Likely they will refuse. That is fine. Your true purpose is to demonstrate to the judge that you tried including your ex-spouse in the decision, but they refused to participate. Be prepared for your ex-spouse's argument that your child does not need therapy. Know the reasons you believe your child does need this support. If you are having difficulty articulating your concerns, schedule your *own* therapy appointment. No one can deny you that. Ask your own therapist to help you formulate your arguments. Then, when you respond to your ex-spouse's arguments, explain why therapy will help your child cope with each of their specific issues. Write, for example, "John, you know that Julie's school work has deteriorated over the past few months and that she is moodier than usual. I believe she is having difficulty accepting our divorce and therapy will provide her a safe place to discuss her feelings about both of us." Such an email accomplishes several goals. First, it assumes your ex-spouse is aware that your child's behavior has changed. If your ex-spouse really is conscious of that fact, then the burden shifts to them to find a way to help your child. If they are unaware of your child's struggles, they are not likely to admit that, especially to the judge. Thus, you have manipulated your ex-spouse into a position of having to "agree" with your assessment or appear like an uninvolved parent. If your ex-spouse elects a third "solution," such as grounding your child until their grades improve, you can argue to the judge that your ex-spouse is punishing your child for reacting to a major life-changing event over which they had no control. Therapy is a kinder and gentler way to help your child adjust.

The second effect of your email is that it allows your ex-spouse to "save face." By including yourself as part of the "problem," your ex-spouse is less likely to feel that you are blaming them for your child's struggles. Leveling the playing field by suggesting your child might need to discuss their feelings about both parents allows them to fantasize that *you* are the source of your child's problems. This notion can tantalize an angry and vindictive ex-spouse and they might agree to therapy, hoping that they will be vindicated, and you will be deemed the source of all the family's problems. It is unlikely that your ex-spouse will verbalize such feelings, but your email would appeal to their ego in service of your child's needs.

If possible, get your child into therapy before a complaint for divorce is filed. Before the court assumes jurisdiction over you and your children, either parent has the legal right to have a minor child seen by a therapist. If you start your child in therapy after the divorce is filed, the judge may punish you for doing something the other parent objected to. But it is much easier to convince a judge to allow a child to remain in therapy that has already begun. Even if your ex-spouse testifies that they opposed the therapy, the judge is unlikely to want to disrupt the status quo. In your argument to the judge, you can even acknowledge that your ex-spouse was reluctant to start therapy, but that therapy *is*, in fact, helping your child. Argue in favor of consistency and stability, and you are more likely to win. "It would not be in your child's best interest to disrupt the ongoing therapeutic relationship," should be your mantra.

This is what I call **the train has left the station** strategy. Judges are parents, too, and they should understand that disrupting therapy that has already begun may be harmful to the child. This strategy may also work *after* the complaint for divorce has been filed. Heather's ex-husband's new wife, Amanda, knew her stepson needed therapy.

He and her own son attended the same school, and she had observed her stepson for several years. Amanda knew that the boy's mother denied that her son was struggling to cope with his parents' divorce. After Amanda married the boy's father, she enlisted the school social worker to help the boy get the support he needed. Amanda and the social worker agreed to enroll the boy in a support group during school. It was a small thing that did not disrupt Heather's schedule, so she agreed.

Later, after consulting with Amanda, the social worker wrote letters to both parents suggesting they consult with a certain therapist. The father, who had been forewarned about this, immediately made an appointment. Following that initial interview, he asked the therapist to invite Heather for a separate interview. The letter noted that a copy was also sent to the school social worker. Heather, who had resisted therapy for her son, now agreed because third parties – the therapist and the social worker – were advising her to consent and she did not want to appear inadequate before third-party professionals. Personality-disordered parents are motivated by preserving their **Public Persona** and you can leverage that to help your child adjust. Amanda and Heather's ex-husband understood that Heather was more motivated by how she appeared to others than by her son's needs. By enlisting others to include Heather – asking *them* to invite her to *hop onto the train just as it was leaving the station* – they secured her consent, knowing she would not want to feel left behind. Enlisting the aid of people who are part of your child's world can help you achieve your goals. In Amanda's case, both the social worker and the therapist understood Heather's reluctance. Amanda and her husband were open and honest about the problem. But both professionals agreed to help because they were asked to include the mother, not exclude her. They were not asked to do anything contrary to their ethics.

Once the reluctant parent has met the social worker or therapist, it becomes more difficult for them to argue that the child does not need therapy. Having met a therapist, they have demonstrated they are at least willing to consider therapy. You now have an opportunity to deflect the conversation with the judge from whether therapy is necessary, to whether your ex-spouse objects to *this* therapist. Do not accept a blanket and unsubstantial answer, such as "I just didn't like him." Ask for specifics and counter with the reasons you do like that therapist, such as by listing the therapist's credentials. Do your best to direct the conversation to the terms of the therapy, rather than to the issue of whether therapy is necessary. The "terms" can always be changed later with a recommendation from the therapist. Whether a child needs braces is another chronic source of conflict. Before requesting your ex-spouse pay their share, invite them to your meeting with the dentist. Keep a record of your invitation, especially if they fail to show up. If they do appear and continue arguing that your child does not need braces, invite them to get a second opinion. Let them know that you want to attend that meeting. Again, preserve these communications. Bring your child's X-rays to the second meeting because your insurance is not likely to pay for two sets of X-rays. On the off chance the second orthodontist agrees with your ex-spouse, ask for a third opinion as a "tie breaker." Should you have to secure a court order allowing your child to get braces and requiring your ex-spouse to pay, you will have plenty of documentation proving that your child needs the procedure and that you made every effort to include your ex-spouse in the decision-making process. You will appear *reasonable,* and your ex-spouse will not.

Unfortunately, even if you have an order, it does not guarantee your ex-spouse will pay their share of the cost. Many **payor** parents in high-conflict cases refuse to pay for their children's needs, even if court ordered to do so. Added to the challenge is the fact that medical service providers require parents or guardians to sign an agreement to pay whatever costs insurance fails to cover, prior to treatment. Thus, the **payee** parent signs a legal contract, knowing they may never be reimbursed by the ex-spouse. Amanda chose to provide braces for her daughter even though she *knew* her ex-husband was not likely to pay. In fact, he told their daughter that daddy was not required to pay for them because she "got them on Mommy's time." Another option is to ask the orthodontist to bill both you and your former spouse. It is possible, although unlikely, that your former spouse will pay the orthodontist directly rather than give the money to you. Finally, you can choose to deprive your child of necessary but "optional" medical care. Unfortunately, there is no anticipating the lies and distortions a personality-disordered parent will use to serve their own interests.

Make your power play regarding health care expenses early on. As soon as sufficient sums have accrued making it cost effective to file a legal action to collect unpaid support, do so. By taking action, you set the ground rules, letting your ex-spouse know that you will not tolerate financial irresponsibility. Some states require a motion be filed to recoup unpaid medical expenses. Others established bureaucratic procedures. Before filing any paperwork, however, take the following measures:

- ❖ Secure from the medical provider a letter or statement verifying the need for treatment.
- ❖ Secure from the medical provider a complete invoice of both the amounts you have paid, and the balance still owed.
- ❖ If you have a court order requiring the medical treatment and requiring your ex-spouse to contribute financially, include a copy of the order with these documents.
- ❖ Send a copy of the letter, invoice and order to your ex-spouse asking them to pay their share. Send it **return-receipt-requested** so that you can verify that your ex-spouse received it.
- ❖ One week later, send a follow-up email asking for confirmation from your ex-spouse that they will pay their share.

If the response you receive asks legitimate questions, refer your ex-spouse directly to the health care provider. You are not the provider and you do not want to be facilitating or managing the relationship between your ex-spouse and your child's doctor.

What you are building is a case showing that your child *needs* the medical treatment; that you are attempting to include your ex-spouse in the process; and that your ex-spouse is not acting in your child's best interests. There are several possible outcomes. First, your ex-spouse refuses to respond. If that is the case, you interpret their silence as a de-facto consent and ask the court to order them to pay. If they outright reject your request, you have two options. One is to proceed and pay the entire bill yourself. This is a "win" for your ex-spouse because they succeeded in having you pay the entire bill. Do not let that derail you. If your child needs braces, your child will again understand that their other parent is not looking out for them. Ultimately, it will be *your* "win."

Your final option is to seek court approval for the procedure and an order requiring your ex-spouse to pay their share. If you seek an order asking the court to approve the medical procedure, you risk losing. But if you proceed to provide the braces for your child and, six months later, you ask the court to order your ex-spouse to pay, you may be able to use the **train has left the station** argument. Wait six months or so before filing your motion. During that time, if you can, send emails informing your ex-spouse of the progress your child is making. Make the emails benign and casual. You are simply keeping them apprised of the situation – no need for a response. Ideally, ask your ex-spouse to take your child to at least one appointment. Then, when you go to court, you can explain that while your ex-spouse initially objected, for the past few months they tacitly agreed. Be prepared for your ex-spouse's rage. There is also a chance the court may punish you for your **self-help**. But the doctor's medical diagnosis will help justify your actions and you can plead ignorance, claiming you thought your ex-spouse was simply posturing because they did not want to pay and you are willing to pay one hundred percent, although that seems unfair. It is unlikely a court will order a child's braces to be removed and, while you may lose your bid to have your ex-spouse pay their share, you are no worse off than you were before your court action, when you knew there was a chance you might end up paying one hundred percent of the medical cost anyway.

When parents share legal custody, they are supposed to agree about providing these medical treatments for their children. Often, a hostile ex-spouse refuses because they do not want to admit there is a problem or because they do not want to pay. While judges prefer being asked ahead of time for permission to provide your children with the medical service, you risk the court saying no. Then, if you attempt to provide it for them, you risk being held in contempt for violating the court order. Judges do not like you to disrespect them. Nor do they like you to **self-help**, but that might be the lesser of two evils. If you strategize carefully, you may be able to get tacit agreement from your ex-spouse. If so, then you can direct the conversation before the court to payment, rather than approval.

Be aware that even if you secure a court order requiring your ex-spouse to reimburse you for the medical expenses, you may not see any of that money unless the court agrees to another wage-withholding order. Your ex-spouse is not a person willing to pay for things you think your children need. A court order may not change that perspective. Furthermore, collecting on judgments is exceedingly difficult; sometimes more difficult than winning the original lawsuit. People are good at hiding money, and hostile ex-spouses who do not want to pay are especially good at doing so.

EXTRA-CURRICULAR AND EXTRA EXPENSES

Unfortunately, enrolling your children in extracurricular activities requires cooperation from your ex-spouse. Most activities will fall on both parent's time, so you will need your ex-spouse to agree to participate. Your ex-spouse, therefore, has tremendous control because they can refuse to allow your children to participate in an activity on their time. Or they can refuse to pay.

If your children are already involved in activities during the divorce, then include those activities – as well as activities you believe they might want to participate in later – in your court order. Use language that acknowledges that these activities are important to your children and that both parents agree to use best efforts to support your children's ongoing participation.

When your children want to participate in a new activity, you will need to secure agreement from your ex-spouse. If your children are old enough, have them ask that parent directly. Your ex-spouse is more likely to respond positively to them than they are to you. If they agree, send a confirming email. If not, there may be nothing more you can do unless you can enroll the children on your time alone.

While judges recognize that extracurricular activities are important, they are often hesitant to order a parent to allow their children to participate in an activity that the other parent opposes. Some judges might order the children to participate in an activity of the judge's choosing. Others might order the parents to select alternate activities every other season. Still others might require the parents to resolve this issue with a mediator or parent coordinator. None of these solutions are ideal. If you find yourself in this type of situation, encourage your children to continue advocating for themselves with their other parent. Your children's relationship with their other parent is life-long, and it behooves them to learn how to manage it.

If you believe that the other parent's reluctance to allow your children to participate in an activity is because it would inconvenience them, perhaps they cannot leave work early to chauffer then children from school to the activity, you have two options. One is to find a carpool and arrange to drive the children on your time. The other is to have the children participate in school-related activities that require them to remain in the building longer, rather than activities that require your ex-spouse to drive them to a distant location.

Changing the driving times to and from school might be more palatable to a reluctant parent than adding more time in the car.

If your ex-spouse consistently refuses to participate in your children's extracurricular activities, your children will quickly learn which parent supports them and which does not. Should you decide you need to get a court order requiring your ex-spouse to allow your children to participate in extracurricular activities – perhaps because they need to bolster their college application – first send an email explaining to your ex-spouse what your children want and why you believe it is necessary. Be factual and concise. Ask your ex-spouse to respond in 48 hours. Regardless of whether they respond or answer negatively, ignore the vitriol, and offer to arrange transportation for your children both to and from the activity when it occurs on their parenting time. Again, ask for a response within 48 hours. After the 48 hours have passed, you will have evidence supporting your children's wishes, your ex-spouse's refusals, and your efforts to cooperate. Include these communications with your **motion,** along with statements from several local colleges and universities admission pages outlining admission requirements. Most include some extracurricular activities. Finally, provide a graph or some other visual aid demonstrating how little the extracurricular activity will interfere with your ex-spouse's parenting time. If, for some reason, the activity is very intrusive, then in court *verbally* offer to relinquish some of your own parenting time. Acknowledge that while you are reluctant to do so you will if it is the only way. If you have proven to the judge that the activity is necessary for your children's future (it provides leadership or community service opportunities, for example), the judge is less likely to accept your sacrifice and will, instead, order your ex-spouse to cooperate.

If you chose not to go to court and there is absolutely no support from your ex-spouse, you may not be able to get reimbursed for extracurricular-related costs unless these costs are included in your child support order as discussed above. When seeking reimbursement, retain copies of all receipts. Once a month, send an invoice to your ex-spouse. Outline the activity, the total cost, and their portion. Include copies of the receipts. Include medical invoices as well. If your ex-spouse has paid any portion, note that on the invoice. Include any outstanding balance. Keep a copy of the entire packet for your records. If your ex-spouse refuses to pay all or a portion of the invoice, identify the outstanding balance on the next invoice. Wait until the amount accrues to the point where it is cost-effective to sue for reimbursement. But do not wait too long. There is a court doctrine called **laches** that states if you have waited too long to act, it must not have been important to you. Courts have, on occasion, dismissed support reimbursement actions for **laches**. On the other hand, if your ex-spouse consistently pays only a portion of the amount due so that it is not cost effective for you to sue them, maintain records of the percentage they paid. When you go to court then, you may be able to defeat a **laches** argument by explaining that your ex-spouse has consistently paid only a percentage of each bill. By charting the percentage paid for each invoice, you can demonstrate a pattern of non-payment that explains why you waited for a sufficient balance to accumulate before you took legal action.

WHEN YOUR SPOUSE IS HIDING INCOME

It is easier for people who own their own business to hide income by failing to claim cash as income than for people who work for a third party. Your self-employed ex-spouse has more control over reported income and reported debt, and they have a greater ability to hide cash. Unfortunately, if you signed the income tax returns with the artificially deflated income, you cannot exact revenge by reporting your ex-spouse to the IRS. By signing the tax return, you affirmed that you agreed with the report. You may not later claim to be an innocent spouse.

Nor is it worth hiring a private detective to photograph your ex-spouse spending more money than they claim to have earned. Your best approach to demonstrating to the judge that your ex-spouse is hiding income is to compile evidence of your combined expenditures during the past year (credit card statements, hotel bills, etc.) and show the judge how everything had been paid off. Compare that to your ex-spouse's reported income, and the discrepancy should be blatant enough to convince the judge that they are hiding income. This is a time-consuming process as you must do all the legwork to collect the evidence. Presenting it to the judge in an understandable and accessible manner is also challenging. There is always the chance you will not be successful. Another option is to simply walk away. Your former spouse may not pay you sufficient child support for you to buy your children's clothes, but hopefully they are buying the clothes themself. If not, then at a minimum, you have more evidence that your ex-spouse is failing to parent the children. Your children will see this and understand.

FILING FEDERAL INCOME TAX

Before the judgment of divorce is finalized, you and former your spouse will continue filing your federal income taxes jointly. That is because you are still married. Once the judgment of divorce is signed, an issue arises as to which parent may claim the minor children as dependents on their federal income tax returns.

Under federal law, the custodial parent is entitled to take the minor children as dependents for all tax purposes. Judgments of divorce, however, often allocate the federal dependency exemption to the non-custodial parent. These judgments, products of state law, conflict with federal law. To comply with federal law, the parent taking the deduction must obtain a signed Form 8332 from the other, which must then be filed with their federal income tax forms. In high-conflict divorce cases, this can pose a problem as it requires the parents to communicate, and it affords one parent the opportunity to demand a "price" for signing the form. If you are the parent entitled to the exemption, keep copies of the email exchanges in which your ex-spouse refused to sign the form. Your options are to take the deduction anyway and risk an audit from the IRS, or to file a motion for contempt in the state court.

UNPAID SUPPORT AND CONTEMPT

If you have a temporary child support order during your divorce and your ex-spouse has failed to pay or owes you money, consult with your attorney about preserving the unpaid support in your final judgment of divorce. If there is an arrearage of child support payments, medical expenses, etc., the judgment of divorce must contain a provision preserving this arrearage. The same provision holds true for any monies owing under any temporary order. If the arrearage is not preserved in the judgment of divorce, it is canceled.

Once the final child support order is entered and your ex-spouse owes you money, you will need to file a motion asking the judge to cite your ex-spouse for **contempt of court**. In most courts, filing a motion for contempt of court is a two-part process, like filing a motion to modify custody or parenting time. First you must file a **motion to show cause**. This motion asks the court to demand that your ex-spouse present themself and justify why they have not paid what they were ordered to pay. Once you are before the court, the court will then determine whether an order was violated. If it was, there will be a second hearing to determine what your ex-spouse owes.

Suing your ex-spouse for unpaid child support may not give you the results you want. Your ex-spouse will arrive at court with a reasonable-sounding excuse the judge may accept. They may ask for more time to pay you, which the judge might agree to. Or they may ask that the amount owed be reduced. Finally, even if you are successful and the judge finds your ex-spouse in contempt, they may still refuse to pay. Remember that you are not dealing with an honorable person, but someone whose self-interests outweigh the needs of their children. Still, you are making a power play and letting your ex-spouse know that you are watching and that at any time you may act. Occasionally, that may be enough to convince your ex-spouse to behave appropriately; but not likely in high-conflict cases.

CHAPTER EIGHT:

D
ividing property in divorce is all about trading one asset of value for another of equal value. That requires valuing property and debt. Some things are easy to value; others create conflict. Savings, investment, and retirement accounts are easy to value by simply reviewing monthly statements. W-2 Wage and Tax Statements reflect a person's wages, unless one of the parties is self-employed, in which case the form may not be accurate. The value of cars is often derived from the Kelley Blue Book. If a couple owns jewelry or art, they might already have appraised these items for insurance purposes. If not, they may hire an appraiser – or two – or resolve this issue.

Some couples can divide their personal property (including clothing and furniture) without court intervention. Others often disagree about the value of their assets, such as their home, and each person hires an appraiser to value the property. If the two appraisals yield vastly different results, there may be a hearing to arrive at the "correct" value of the home. Or this matter might be resolved at trial. Chris, who had moved out of the family home, hired an expert to appraise everything he and his wife owned. She was humiliated standing aside while the appraiser opened cupboards and drawers to appraise her things. She did not challenge the value he ascribed to their belongings and Chris claimed his half share. That meant if she kept certain property, she had to give up something of equal value. In her case, she received less cash – equivalent to the value of the dining room table – because she kept the table.

The default position of most courts is that property should be divided equally. Divorce courts, as courts of equity or justice, may find that while fifty percent is equal, it is not equitable or fair. Most people feel that wrongdoers should be punished. They believe it is fair if the abusing or personality-disordered spouse receive less property from the divorce. Proving otherwise, that you deserve more of the assets or less of the debt is often a matter of fairness. On the other hand, the personality-disordered spouse who feels victimized by the divorce, even if they left you, is certain they deserve the bulk of the assets. An ex-spouse who will sacrifice the children to win the divorce, will also sacrifice or consume all the marital assets by fighting to keep them.

Dividing assets is not always as easy as deciding who gets which television, although that, too, can cause conflict. Some couples have such difficulty dividing up personal property that they end up in mediation because judges are reluctant to get involved in such minutia. But keep in mind that different assets have different debt and tax consequences associated with them. Withdrawing early from a retirement account to purchase half of the value of the house incurs penalties. These factors must be considered. Do not rely on your attorney unless they are a certified financial adviser. If you are not confident in your own ability to evaluate the pros and cons of which asset to keep and which to trade, spend the money to meet with a financial adviser. If you prepare well, you should only need one visit. Bring to the meeting accurate statements of your income and your budget. Bring current statements of all your financial accounts and marital debt. Finally, bring the agreed-upon appraised value of your primary assets (house, boat, etc.). Organize all the information you have and have a decent idea of what is important for you to keep and what you are willing to relinquish. Within an hour or two, a good financial adviser should be able to help you understand the pros and cons of your options.

Like all negotiations or mediations, prepare in advance before you propose or respond to an offer. This will require you to spend time considering where you see yourself five years after the divorce. Will you be living in the same home? Will you be working at the same job? Will your children still be living with you, or will some have graduated high school and moved out? You should also take this time to consider whether there are things in your life you have always wanted to do but could not. Are some possible now? These questions will help you identify what assets are important to you and what you may be willing to give up. If your children will be leaving home soon and you have always wanted to travel, for example, then perhaps keeping an expensive house is not the best plan. If you prefer keeping the house and have many years to build retirement savings, then perhaps you can relinquish your IRA in exchange for your ex-spouse's share of the house's equity. The take-home point is to know your priorities. Know what you really need, what you want, and what you are willing to give up. But never give those assets up too easily. Always get something in exchange, preferably something you want or need.

THE HOUSE

Before the judgment of divorce is finalized, a decision needs to be made about the marital home. Most people want to remain in their home. The issues surrounding the house are financial and emotional. Because the house is often a couple's largest asset and is mortgaged, it presents a unique set of problems. Transferring the mortgage presents tremendous problems in a high-conflict divorce. And because the marital home represents the security of family, most people are extremely attached to it and do not want to lose it. But it will be expensive to maintain and not always affordable.

Often the home is awarded to the custodial parent, which is more often the mother than the father. That decision is made to reduce the amount of disruption the children experience during their parent's divorce. The parent who remains in the home faces several issues. First, the ex-spouse will be given time to collect their things. When this happens, ask the court to order a third party to be present. This is to reduce the opportunity for an angry ex-spouse to destroy property before walking out the door. Another tactic used by angry ex-spouses is to repeatedly file motions asking to return to the house to collect things they "forgot." In that situation, ask the judge for an order requiring the ex-spouse to draft a final, comprehensive list of items and that anything not taken in one visit is "lost." Again, have a third person be present to check items off the list.

If you decide you want the house, you will need to "purchase" or trade your ex-spouse's share of the equity. One way is to give up an equal value of cash from a savings or retirement account. Remember that early withdrawal from retirement accounts will cost you an additional penalty. If you do not have sufficient assets to exchange for their share of the equity, you will have to refinance. Before deciding to keep the house consider whether you have sufficient income to support the new mortgage. In either case, you will have to remove your ex-spouse's name from the first mortgage.

Another issue with keeping the house is the title and mortgage. If you keep the house, your ex-spouse will need to sign a **Quit Claim Deed** giving you full title to the house. Despite a court order, many people in these high-conflict cases refuse to do that. Do not be surprised if your ex-spouse, while demanding that you refinance or remove their name from the mortgage, also refuse to sign title of the house over to you. Their stance is illogical because you cannot get a mortgage until you have title to the house. But like all personality-disordered people, their mind will disconnect these two conflicting demands. You may continue paying the mortgage and hope that one day you can secure the title. Another option is to refuse to sign over the title to the car or any other asset belonging to them until they sign the deed of the house over to you. You can also withhold the money you owe them in exchange for the equivalent value of their half of the house. Or you can return to court with a **motion for show cause** asking the judge to order your ex-spouse to appear before them and explain why they refuse to sign a quit claim deed awarding you full title to the house. Should you choose this option, bring a partially complete deed with you to court and ask the judge to order your ex-spouse to sign it immediately.

Unfortunately, an even bigger problem exists if your ex-spouse continues living in the house while you remain on the mortgage. You, too, will be liable for the mortgage payment if your ex-spouse fails to make the monthly payments or maintain the property according to the terms of your mortgage. If you decide to relinquish the house to your ex-spouse, they must "purchase" your share of the equity. You will face the same problems from the opposite perspective. In this scenario, link *your* willingness to sign the **Quit Claim Deed** with their willingness to refinance the mortgage. They cannot refinance until you sign, but you will not sign until they are ready to refinance. Agree to sign the deed on the date they refinance the mortgage and attend the closing. In that way, you will know for certain that they refinanced your mortgage.

A third option is for the two of you to sell the house together. Again, in high-conflict cases this raises other issues, such as whether both parties are doing enough to sell the house. I know of one man who vandalized his own home so it could not be sold without a lot of costly repairs, simply because he was angry with his ex-wife.

When considering what to do with the house, remember to strategize. First, consider if you can afford the house. Consider the mortgage, insurance, and maintenance costs. Also consider the sentimental value of the house. Is it the four walls that you value or is it that this is the place where you celebrated wonderful family Christmas parties together? Is it the structure or the community? Could you replace the structure while maintaining the community? If so, then trading the house in exchange for a liquid asset, such as a greater percentage of your combined investment account, might be the right choice for you.

Second, if you do choose to relinquish the house, carefully consider what you want in exchange. Consider whether there are sufficient assets in the savings, investment, and retirement accounts and what type of money you need most. Do you need to build your savings or retirement account? If there are insufficient liquid assets, your ex-spouse must refinance the house. The house is a terrific bargaining tool simply because your ex-spouse wants it.

Third, your first negotiating position should be to *demand* the house, knowing you are making that demand solely for leverage since you have already decided to give it up. Your second negotiating position is to demand that the house be sold. If you have already chosen to give up the house, then selling it is a win-win, as you will not remain liable on the mortgage while your ex-spouse continues living in the house. If your former spouse really *wants* the house, however, they will have more incentive to refinance if their only other option is to sell.

Some couples agree to keep the house until the youngest child is eighteen. They would then sell the house and each capture half the increased equity. In a high-conflict divorce, this plan keeps the parties engaged. They will be required to interact with each other to guarantee that the mortgage and insurance are being paid and the home is properly maintained. The possibility of ongoing conflict is high and would undermine the notion that keeping the house provides security for the children.

If you purchase a new home, consider a house in which the mortgage is no more than the cost of an apartment. If you are receiving spousal support, it is likely your income will *decline* once that support stops. When budgeting for housing, then, consider your cash flow during your worst economic times, knowing it is easier to upgrade than to be forced to downgrade even further because of poor planning.

One last issue facing the spouse who keeps the house is where the ex-spouse will live. For the sake of the children, it is best if the parents do not live too far apart. The closer they are the less time everyone must spend in the car. But they should not live too close either. Gary wanted to buy the house across the street from his ex-wife. She lived on a hill and could see into the living room of that house as she descended her driveway. She did not want to be reminded of him every time she left or returned home. She *was* able to convince him that this was too close, and he instead chose to buy a house on the other side of town, far from her home, which created other problems. Heidi's ex-husband, on the other hand, bought a house on a street around the corner from her. That was ideal for the kids to have both parents living in the same neighborhood, but Heidi did not need to pass his house every day on the way to and from her own.

DEBT

Dividing debt involves a similar process as dividing assets. The general rule is that the person who takes the property takes the debt associated with it. If the wife is awarded the house, for example, she also assumes the mortgage. If the husband is awarded his Lexus, he also assumes responsibility for the car loan. More painful are the debts for which there is no associated asset, such as credit card debt. That is usually divided equally or can be traded for another asset. Meghan loved her home and had spent a lot of time and money decorating it. But she and her husband had lived far beyond their means and had accumulated tremendous debt. After much painful soul searching, she ultimately agreed to give him the house, not only in exchange for being released from the mortgage, but also for his assumption of all their unsecured (credit card) debt.

Debt accumulated during marriage is presumed to be marital debt. Even debt accumulated because of the wife's girls' weekend at the spa and the husband's boys' trip to Vegas are considered marital because the other spouse sanctioned the events. Money spent on extramarital affairs is not, of course, marital debt. Finally, if one person is less concerned about the debt or has greater earning power, the other should try to exchange the debt for an asset. It is easier to re-accumulate assets without burdensome debt than to try rebuilding your life while digging yourself out from a mountain of pre-divorce debt.

SPOUSAL SUPPORT

Spousal support is now considered to be **rehabilitative**. It is short term and designed to get a person back on their feet post-divorce. The most common rationale for spousal support is to help a person retrain themselves for better prospects in the job market. If you were not working during the last few years of your marriage, or you are unhappy with your chosen career, your divorce is a time to re-evaluate. Spend time researching your prospects and present them to the court, asking that your ex-spouse support you as you had supported them. If you had worked while your spouse attended school, then your argument is especially strong. It is only fair that your ex-spouse supports your education efforts because you supported theirs. Present a reasonable plan and, if your ex-spouse vehemently opposes it, ask the court to have them pay your tuition directly. They may find it more palatable to pay a third party than pay you directly.

Another option is to bargain for a greater portion of the marital property, enough to cover your education. Spousal support is taxable to the receiving party and deductible to the **payor**, whereas the transfer of marital property is tax neutral. By taking a greater amount of cash, you may have enough to pay your tuition without having to pay income tax.

Finally, it is imperative to preserve whatever spousal support you receive. Your support is finite. It will end and if you consume that money as well as your wages, your standard of living will suddenly deteriorate after the last payment is made. Instead, live as well as possible on your income and preserve as much as you can of your spousal support. Use it sparingly so that it can continue supplementing your income *after* it terminates.

CHAPTER NINE:

I n a high-conflict divorce, email is a trap. Never forget that every email you write to your ex-spouse can and will be read by the court. With that in mind, always write thinking that the judge will be looking over your shoulder. Always leave a positive email trail.

The difficulty comes in remaining positive while your ex-spouse is pushing all your buttons, demanding unreasonable accommodations, or falsely accusing you. *Never respond immediately.* Unless it is a life-and-death situation (and email is rarely used in those circumstances), wait until you calm down before drafting your response. Do not allow your former spouse to manipulate you into writing something they will later use against you in court. Also be cognizant that email and phone calls are requests for attention, not demands. Remember that not every call for attention requires you to respond. Recognize that some emails are sent for the sole purpose of engaging you. If that is the case, become a *black hole*. You do not need to answer every email you receive, especially if the purpose is to engage you in another meaningless fight.

It is often difficult to identify the *real* purpose of the email because the presenting issue seems legitimate. Perhaps your ex-wife is asking that when you bring your son to her house you also bring his hockey helmet because the helmet at her house has broken. This seems like a reasonable request, but *you* know the history: she consistently refused to pay her share of the hockey participation fees and cost of the equipment, and instead purchased an inadequate helmet on E-Bay. You had argued with her in the past about your son's safety and at every game you bring the better helmet to protect him from concussions. But you will not be able to attend this game and now *she* wants the better helmet. Your first emotional response to the seemingly reasonable email, then, is anger. If you need to, get a reality check from someone you trust. Have them read the email and validate – and perhaps help you articulate – what you suspect is wrong with the content of the email you just received. Remember that your ex-spouse is an expert at appearing reasonable. Sometimes it is difficult understanding exactly *why* their request riled you.

The first thing to do is draft the email response you want to send, but never will send. An important note: before you do this, *remove the address* so that if you accidentally hit send, the email will go into your draft file and will not be sent. In this draft email, liberally express all the reasons why you despise your ex-spouse and why you refuse to capitulate. Let out all your anger and tension. Not only will this be cathartic, it will also help you clarify the real issues. But remember not to hit send.

DRAFTING YOUR RESPONSE

If there is a substantive purpose to the email, you must answer it. Failing to do so makes you appear uncooperative. Your task will be to determine the real issue behind the lies, accusations, and insults, and then prepare an appropriate response. Writing an appropriate response takes much time, effort, and strategizing. Email is very time-consuming and slipping up can be costly.

Start by determining whether a response is needed at all. Sometime no response is a response. By carefully selecting which emails you will respond to – those that raise substantive issues versus those that are simply designed to engage – you teach your ex-spouse you will not jump whenever they say so. Just because they demand your attention via email does not mean they are entitled to it. You are the keeper of your time and can select how you want to spend it and with whom you want to spend it. That includes time spent on emails.

Next, outline your response on a separate page. What does your ex-spouse want and why? What do you want and why? Why would you refuse your ex-spouse or why are they refusing you? These questions should help you get to the root of the issue. When you were married, even if you fought a lot, eventually the two of you found a way to cut through all the emotion and reach the heart of an issue. You may have screamed and yelled, but ultimately the message got through. Now you no longer talk and do not live together, even if you are still sleeping under the same roof. Recognize that, depending on how long you have been physically and/or emotionally separated, you no longer know the other person as well as you once did. It used to be that you could decipher their moods by their body language. You understood they were having a bad week because they told you about how boss was on the rampage. Now you no longer have access to that information. Nor do you really know what thoughts are going through your former spouse's head. You can assume their basic personality has not changed, but you cannot assume you know them in the same way as when you were married. Your task then, is to discern what they are *really* asking for or trying to accomplish, and this takes careful consideration.

Next consider what you would be willing to agree to. How much will you bend? Never forget that every interaction is a negotiation, and the rule of negotiation is to start by knowing what you will give up and what you will never give up. Know your limits.

Do not respond to every misstatement or issue raised or you will appear defensive. Instead, determine which issue or issues you are willing to negotiate or agree to. These issues do not have to be the issues raised by your ex-spouse. In fact, they might be entirely different because, after having drafted your outline on a separate page, you may have clarity on what the *real* issue is, understanding that your ex-spouse lacks insight and self-awareness. In other words, your ex-spouse might be yelling at you for being "unreasonably angry" when they returned the kids late, but you now understand the real issue is that they hate being accountable to you or the court. Knowing that, you can reframe the issue and negotiate, or take control by taking the moral high ground. You could write, for example, "I appreciate that you are sensitive to the time constraints of your parenting time, and I know you make every effort to bring the children home on time." What can they say to this? They have accused you of being irrationally angry and you have turned the conversation back to them without making accusations or being defensive. Imagine how sensitive that response sounds to a judge?

Another option is to respond to an entirely different question. You can say, for example, "I appreciate that you have difficulty getting the children back on time. I, too, struggle with delivering them to you on time as well. Can you propose a solution?" Will they respond with a proposal? If so, you do not have to agree, and you should not agree unless, after careful consideration, they *have* proposed something workable. But chances are that they will not respond because they *really do not want to work with you*. They simply want to regain control through the only way they know how: by bullying you. By asking for their input, you may silence them. But you are more likely to have changed the dialogue away from attacking you. Where it goes next is irrelevant. To the court, it would appear that you have responded appropriately.

I once had an English teacher who, in preparing our class to take the Advanced Placement exam, told us that if we do not know the answer to the question, answer a different question. "What question?" we wanted to know. "Whatever you choose," he responded. I have never forgotten this conversation, recalling that the examiners were looking for logic and grammar, not necessarily a specific answer. That is not always the case, of course, but you do not need to accept your ex-spouse's agenda. You can create your own.

Resist the temptation to explain yourself. Never forget that your ex-spouse is not at all interested in you, your feelings, or your rationale. Just the opposite, in fact. If you reveal that something is important to you, you have given them information that can be used against you. If you say, for example, that you want Brittany to be well so she can travel with you, you give your ex-spouse the opportunity to exaggerate Brittany's illness and deny your parenting time. Now they can demand, in the interest of Brittany's health, that Brittany stay home and not travel at all with you. Neither of these decisions are your former spouse's. Unless your child is deathly ill, you can take her with you on vacation. But by opening a dialogue, you have invited your ex-spouse to express their opinion. And a disordered person always has an opinion to share.

Never engage in conflict in an email exchange because if you shout (use all capital letters) or swear, you can be certain your ex-spouse will parade that email before the judge. Never be verbally abusive. Stick to the facts and issues. Summarily dismiss their accusations by "feeling their pain." Acknowledge their emotion and then re-direct it. Do not offer too much information because you do not want your ex-spouse to continue the dialogue or to rely on you. You want them to go away.

EXAMPLE ONE

Your ex-spouse sends an email challenging whether your child needs braces, amidst a host of other accusations (such as you are wasting their money on unnecessary procedures). Do not take the bait. Your response can be, "I understand you have concerns. Dr. Ryan can answer them better than me. Here is his number." In this way, you have responded, refused to engage, and appear cooperative to the court. If the issue is ever raised in court, you can point out that you informed your ex-spouse how to manage the situation and, if they chose not to do anything, then doesn't that demonstrate they are not quite the good a parent they claim to be?

You may choose not to provide your ex-spouse with the orthodontist's telephone number. Be cautious. If they are accustomed to relying on you to provide all the parenting information and you no longer wish to do that, let them know in that email that they will have to acquire the information themselves, and keep the email so you have a record of that conversation.

EXAMPLE TWO

Your divorce is not finalized yet your former spouse accuses you of spending too much on the children. They want you to reimburse them. In fact, you did spend too much but you are not able to pay them back. One possible response is: "I will have to look into exactly how much I spent. In the meantime, have your lawyer send me the exact amount you believe I owe with an explanation. Thanks." In other words, make them do the work himself. Do not work for them. Also, by suggesting that their lawyer do the work, they will have to spend money if they really want this accounting. Either way, they are less likely to pursue the matter if you are not going to play the game. If they do take another shot at collecting from you, however, and send a follow-up email demanding, for example, that you produce the receipts, you can say, "I'm really busy at work right now and we can manage this at the final accounting or at trial." Once again if the judge reads the email, you appear agreeable and respectful, albeit not focused.

EXAMPLE THREE

Your ex-spouse wants to take the kids to see the opening of a new movie next weekend but learns that you have made plans to take them yourself on the Thursday before. They send you an angry email accusing you of taking them on Thursday only to hurt them by preventing them from sharing the experience with the children. They accuse you of cruelly using the children to hurt them and demand that you do not go. You can agree, or you can decline in a way that sounds conciliatory: "I am sure the kids would love to see that movie with you. Yes, we already made plans to see it on Thursday night, but I am sure they would love to see it twice. If not, let me know when the next movie opening is, and I will do my best to make sure you have that time." What have you accomplished with this response? First, you validated your ex-spouse's parenting attempt and did not rise to the "bait" that you are using the kids to hurt them. You will appear to the court both respectful and responsive to their concerns: a good co-parent. Second, you offered a vague promise of future behavior that you can choose to follow or not. Unless you have a pattern of pre-empting five or six movie premieres and your ex-spouse is keeping track, you are not likely to get "trapped" by your *intentionally vague promise*. Third, you rejected their "suggestion" that you drop your plans and let *them* take the children to the movie premier instead. You have preserved your time with your children in a way that sounds politely apologetic. And finally, most children *do* like to see movies more than once and who cares if they see it again on the other parent's parenting time? This is a win-win. The children have fun, and you do not have to pay twice.

FOLLOWING UP

It is essential to *always send confirming emails*. If you and your former spouse reach an agreement on the telephone or in person, memorialize your conversation with a confirming email. Otherwise, you enable your ex-spouse to deny the conversation ever took place. Your email can be quite simple: "Just confirming that the emergency room doctor said Brittany will be fine but needs her EpiPen with her at all times." Not only do you remind Brittany's other parent that they must have the pen with him, but if they later refuse to pay the medical bills, you also have evidence that they knew about the emergency room visit.

If you are being pressured in an email to answer definitively about something troublesome to you, or if you are concerned that your response might be used against you but feel you have no choice and must respond, consider trying to resolve the matter on the telephone. Speaking directly is not ideal and should be a last-resort solution, but its advantage is that it leaves no paper trail. But do not immediately pick up the phone and call! You still need a paper trail demonstrating that you *tried* resolving the issue. Your responsive email should be: "We should talk on the phone about this."

Once again, you are in the driver's seat. You have now informed your former spouse *and the court* that you will respond, you have not memorialized that response so that it can be used against you, and you bought yourself more time to prepare. In the movie *The Big Easy*, Ellen Barkin's character prepared a list of issues to discuss with Dennis Quaid. She sat at her desk and crossed off each one as she spoke. The producer used this scene to demonstrate that she was anxious, but I see it differently. Knowing that when a person is stressed, they do not think clearly, and knowing that a bully is adept at misdirecting conversations away from the core issues, it is useful to have your list prepared. If your ex-spouse starts bullying you on the telephone, you are better able to return to the core issues written on your list. You are less likely to "get lost" in a circuitous conversation. If they continue yelling, you can always hang up. Then, send an email saying, "I am sorry you were so angry during our telephone conversation that you had to yell. Call me when you are calm." If they call and yell again, send another email, stating that you do not have to be subjected to their yelling and you will address the matter in court. It is up to you, then, whether to file a motion. If the issue was important to your ex-spouse, they will have to learn to behave properly before you will communicate. Like Pavlov's dog, you are training them to behave appropriately.

CHAPTER TEN:

You have many tools in your toolbox for managing your high-conflict divorce. Court is only one of those tools. However, you see your life "after all this is over," your goal is certainly to regain control over and minimize the amount of money, time, and stress spent responding to your ex-spouse's call for attention. Whether they are prone to calling you and spewing their venom, or they are addicted to litigation, with strategic planning, over time, you can regain control over your life. Like any chess game, you must strategize how you will get to the other side. But unlike chess, you have many different tools. Be mindful of all your tools. Keep them in your "back pocket," so to speak, and like any good carpenter, consider each situation carefully before selecting the right tool for the job.

TO ENGAGE OR NOT TO ENGAGE

It is your choice to engage or not to engage. This is the most difficult decision because the stakes always seem high, especially if the issue involves your children. But what is at stake is not always the issue being presented. Sometimes the children are being used as a vehicle to keep you engaged. Consider whether your ex-spouse enjoys the battle. Consider whether they are someone who needs to win. Consider whether your ex-spouse is being vindictive. If so, then the children's "issue" is merely the tool being used in service to those real goals.

If this is your situation, then your decision about whether to engage or not becomes clearer. On one hand, you are faced with the "issue" being presented, something involving your children. On the other hand, the underlying issue is your ex-spouse's relentless need to keep the war going. Your choice then is whether this battle is worth fighting. If you chose to engage, you may or may not win, depending on the presenting issue. But you will have lost ground in the sense that your ex-spouse's campaign to keep you engaged succeeded yet again. You have reinforced their strategy.

Sometimes you must engage because the cost of doing nothing is too high. But you will never be able to protect your children from every painful decision their other parent makes. So, if you chose not to engage, you have still accomplished two goals. The first is that you are not your ex-spouse's puppet. They cannot manufacture an issue for the purpose of pulling your strings and forcing you to respond. The second is that your children learn the truth about their other parent.

At some point in your children's lives, they will begin understanding who their other parent really is. Most people do not begin to really see their parents as other than "mom" and "dad" until they are adults themselves. But it is a lesson we all learn. If your children learn sooner rather than later, they will be better prepared to cope with that parent throughout their life. If they learn that lesson while living with you, you will be there to help them adjust.

Judges and therapists admonish parents not to denigrate the other parent in front of the children. You need not say anything because often that other parent will bury themselves. Their actions and poor choices will destroy their relationship with their children. You cannot protect your children. But you can teach them how to cope.

Your choices, then, are to engage, knowing that doing so reinforces your ex-spouse's strategy to remain involved and in control of your life; or not to engage, knowing your children will be hurt but knowing you can help them accept their reality and develop coping mechanisms. This may seem harsh but weigh the "issue" de jour against the long-term benefits of refusing to play.

Whatever choice you make, be prepared for the consequences. You know your ex-spouse. You know how they cope with their anger and being mindful of that will help you strategize. Before responding, consider both how you will reply and then brainstorm all their likely reactions. Do a "if this, then that" assessment and use the information to pre-determine your own behavior. Will they call and yell? Will you refuse to pick up the phone? Will they send you endless text messages and, if so, will you try to stop them? How will you do that? Whatever decision you make, be certain to send a "confirming email" acknowledging their anger and firmly – but very briefly – outline your decision. Remember that the judge will be reading your email. Make certain to appear reasonable and responsible. Copy your attorney on that email, but do not send a blind copy. You want your ex-spouse to understand that a third person is monitoring your interactions because you know that your ex-spouse is always conscious of appearing appropriately to others.

If you chose to engage, behave as if you are willing to go to court to resolve the issue. Your objective is to lead them to believe that you are willing to increase the cost of the battle. You may have to litigate once or twice, but by driving up the cost of engaging, your ex-spouse may eventually decide that the money is not worth the fight.

Another strategy to enhance the cost of the battle is to prepare for court but give in at the last moment, perhaps the day before the hearing. Agree at the last minute to what they had wanted. Have you angered them? Certainly. But again, you have taught them that there is a price to pay for unreasonable demands or refusing to compromise. Be self-aware. You may inadvertently be enabling your abusive ex-spouse to continue being abusive, and in the process teach your children to become either the abuser or the abused. Be aware of the difference between what you *want* to provide your children with and what you *need* to provide them with. If what you want is more than they need and beyond your ability to provide, be cautious about asking your ex-spouse to help or participate. After years of physical and emotional abuse, Cynthia finally divorced her husband. Still, the two remained engaged in struggle and conflict. When Cynthia's youngest daughter was twelve, they began preparing for her bat mitzvah. Cynthia lived in a community where children enjoyed very lavish, expensive bar and bat mitzvah parties. Her ex-husband, a successful businessperson, had plenty of money. Cynthia had less. On one hand, she lamented his abusiveness to her and her daughter. On the other hand, she was determined to give her daughter the bat mitzvah party she "deserved." Cynthia believed she was obligated to provide for her daughter what other girls in the community enjoyed, perhaps because she felt guilty for her part in the divorce.

Cynthia did not want her daughter to suffer because of her choices, but she was unable to see that by asking her ex-husband to pay for the lavish affair she was keeping herself and her daughter captive to his abuse. By refusing to consider a smaller party that she could afford without financial assistance, she was allowing him to remain involved in their lives and on his terms because he held the purse strings. Cynthia's ex-husband understood this. His place in the family as ultimate authority, or abuser, remained secure.

Sadly, the party would never be all that Cynthia and her daughter hoped for. They were sharing the event with their abuser. They would smile and pretend everything was wonderful, but there would always be an underlying tension in the room. It is doubtful they could ever fully relax and enjoy themselves. Was the price worth the cost? Did Cynthia sacrifice her and her daughter's self-respect for a party? Only Cynthia can answer that question, but by allowing her ex-husband to be involved while continuing his abuse, Cynthia may have taught her daughter that abuse may be tolerated in exchange for financial reward.

When you remain married to an abusive spouse you teach your children that abuse is acceptable. You teach them there are two roles in a relationship: that of abuser and that of victim. Emma's husband was always late. He worked late into the night and slept late in the morning before leaving for work at noon. They had two small children and family time occurred only when Emma drove to her husband's office, kids in tow, for a late dinner. Then Emma and the kids drove home alone. When they were invited out, Emma and her husband arrived separately because he had other "important" places to be. Had they remained married, Emma would have taught her children it is okay to be disrespectful of other people's time and that it is appropriate to enable the selfish person at the expense of family and friends.

After their divorce, Emma offered her children a stark contrast. She was always on time while her ex-husband continued arriving late, even to the kids' gymnastic competitions and lacrosse games. Sometimes he did not show up at all. By adopting new customs in her own household, Emma taught her children there is another way. Without a word from her, the children learned that what their father did felt bad, and what their mother did felt good. Now, the children are both punctual and conscientious about respecting other people's time.

During your marriage it was often necessary to enable your spouse for the sake of peace. After your divorce, you no longer need to do so. In fact, if you continue enabling your ex-spouse, then you have simply reduced their incentive to cooperate. Because they no longer share a house with you, they can shut out your anger and frustration. At the same time, however, they will continue manipulating you for their own ends. If you disallow that by demonstrating a willingness to occasionally "sacrifice your children," you can eventually change their behavior. Sometimes the sacrifice is small. After the divorce, Emma refused to bring the kids to her ex-husband during his parenting time, forcing him to leave work earlier or miss time with his children. On a larger scale, Cynthia could sacrifice a lavish party to extricate herself and her daughter from her ex-husband's grip. In both cases, the loss to the child is minor relative to the lesson you have taught them – that there is another way to live.

PAVLOV'S DOG: TRAINING YOUR EX-SPOUSE

It is all a power play. If it were not, if your ex-spouse really was thinking of the children, then you would not be in this situation.

Cynthia's daughter would have her party without being subjected to her father's abuse. Emma's husband would be at the kids' activities. And both Cynthia and Emma would be able to discuss the issues surrounding party planning and logistics with their ex-husbands without repercussions. Instead, Cynthia continued living with fear and anxiety long after the divorce while Emma tried to train her ex-spouse. She was not entirely successful as he continued arriving late, but the children learned the value of time. Emma did not disparage her husband but effectively taught the children that his way was not her way. The children chose hers.

Like Pavlov's Dog, you must reward your former spouse's good behavior and punish the bad behavior. You cannot reason or rationalize with them. You cannot explain yourself. They do not listen because they do not care. In high-conflict divorces, your personality disordered former spouse's goal is to keep you engaged. If you fail to engage when they misbehave – yell at you or berate you – but do respond when they behave appropriately, they will eventually learn to treat you properly. Your objective is to train your ex-spouse to understand you will engage only on your own terms.

You are undoubtedly fearful of giving your ex-spouse everything they want with respect to custody of the children. You are worried about your children's emotional well-being and their physical safety. Resist the choice to fight *every* legal battle. Do not let your pride get in the way either. Be mindful about when you engage. Fight the critical issues. Fight the issues that will help you achieve your long-term goals. And occasionally fight when your ex-spouse least expects you to, so they learn you are now a formidable opponent and no longer the person they could once push around.

Training your ex-spouse to use email appropriately takes a long time. Remember that you do *not* need to answer every email; they are requests for your attention. You have the option of not-responding. By selecting which call for attention you answer, you continue training your ex-spouse. If, for example, you never respond to nasty emails but do respond to polite emails, eventually your ex-spouse will learn that the only way to get your attention is by being nice. If you must respond because the issue requires it, do not rise to the bait. Address the issue in a perfunctory and professional manner. Your goal is to teach your ex-spouse that they must be selective about the issues they raise and careful about the way they raise them.

Training your former spouse on the telephone is easier in that you can always hang up. Gary once called his ex-wife and began yelling at her. She hung up and he called right back. The first words out of her mouth were, "Are you ready to stop yelling?" but he was so busy pursuing his own agenda – shouting at her as loudly as he could – that he did not hear. He said, "We got cut off " and returned to yelling. Needless to say, she hung up again. Now all their phone calls, which are exceedingly rare, are pleasant. They both pretend that they are getting along. In a high-conflict divorce, the pretense is as valuable as the reality.

It is critical that you never let your ex-spouse see that they succeeded in angering you. Do not give them that satisfaction. Whenever you are together, at your child's school or in court, always be polite. If you are so inclined, be friendly. Ask about their parents or their job. This will go a long way towards diffusing your conflict. Remember that your disordered ex-spouse is an expert at presenting themself appropriately. They have perfected her **Public Persona,** and this is their usual state of being. This is how they go out into the world. It is their default mode. If you, too, present a **Public Persona** that is polite and even friendly, your disordered ex-spouse may automatically revert to that default mode and be polite to you too. Never forget that deep down your disordered ex-spouse wants you to see them as they see themself. They want to return to that time when you first married, and you accepted them – you actually believed – that they were the person they *want* to be. Your personality disordered former spouse wants to believe that their **Public Persona** is genuine and that you think so, too. What they do *not* want is to look into your eyes and see their **Real Self** – the person you know them to *really* be – the person you divorced. Your disordered ex-spouse wants the reflection of them in your eyes to *be* her **Public Persona**. So, give it to them. When you encounter each other – which you undoubtedly will since you have children together – be polite. If you need to interact with them, act as if they were the person you thought you married. You played the game once. You can do it again. Yes, you are being hypocritical, but remember that if you continue interacting with your ex-spouse as they *really are* rather than as *they want to be*, you will continue inflaming their anger. There is nothing to lose but everything to gain by being two-faced.

Should you agree to meet with your ex-spouse in person, always chose a public, high-traffic location. Again, this subtly encourages them to don their **Public Persona**. Arrive early to manage the physical space. Select a seat in the center of the room that is highly visible and allows you freedom of movement. You want to be in a place where the eyes and ears of strangers are all around you, knowing that your ex-spouse is extremely sensitive to their public appearance.

Your ex-spouse is less likely to scream and shout in public where they can be overheard.

You also want to be able to leave quickly. You do not want to be sitting in a corner with your back against the wall and your ex-spouse blocking your path to escape. If you do need to escape, stand, and loudly announce that you need to use the restroom. Once you are standing, you can either go to the restroom or go to your car. Alternatively, you can "receive an urgent phone call" (having left your cell phone on vibrate) and rush out the door. Finally, if you drive, park your car as close to the entrance as possible and back your car into the space. You do not want to be in a situation where you cannot back out of your parking space because your ex-spouse is standing in the way. Gary once stood in the space inside his ex-wife's open car door so she could not close it and back out without running him over. She was trapped as he continued yelling at her. That happened only once.

Never be trapped in a conversation for which you are unprepared. You should not be pressured into agreeing to something you have not thoroughly considered. Before meeting, know what the issue is and come prepared for how you are going to manage it. Decide what you will agree to and what price, if any, you will exact. Be ready to negotiate. Do not give everything you are willing to relinquish at first. Give a little, then hold out. If your ex-spouse is unwilling to budge, then the negotiation is over. But if you gain ground, then give up what you had previously come prepared to offer to close the deal. It is extremely important to send a confirming email outlining the agreement in case you end up in court over the issue.

If, during your conversation, a new issue is raised for which you are unprepared, remember you need not resolve it immediately. Take your time answering. Their deadline is not your deadline. And unless there is a medical emergency, their time constraint is probably a result of their own delays and failures to act. Never allow your ex-spouse's negligence to trap you into agreeing to something you have not thoroughly thought through. Agree to consider the issue and offer to get back to them. If they show signs that they are getting angry, ask them to share their concerns. Let them talk, and nod as if you are listening. When you finish listening, stand, and say, loudly, "I'll get back to you on that," and leave as quickly as possible.

Do not forget, though, that in high-conflict cases, there is rarely a "bank account;" that is, even though you and your ex-spouse reached agreement on one issue, do not assume you have entered into a new phase of cooperation. Remember, your disordered ex-spouse reflexively rewrites history. They will not remember that you two settled an issue together. In their mind, they still gave up everything and you gave up nothing. Cooperation is not in their repertoire. Thus, it may take years to retrain them.

THE UNPREDICTABILITY DANCE

When you and your spouse lived together, you developed certain communication patterns. Even if you were shouting, you were communicating. Each of you had some incentive, no matter how miniscule, to resolve your issues. Now that you are separated and/or divorced, there is little communication, and you cannot rely on the old dance. You will not accomplish anything, for example, by shouting at your ex-spouse, "Stop bombarding me with email!" In fact, you might encourage them to do that very thing because now they know it irritates you.

Whatever your communication patterns, even if they were unhealthy, they were still your private dance. He came home late for dinner, you yelled, and he reacted with anger. Perhaps you spent too much money at Target, and he tore up your credit cards, so you threw his cell phone into the toilet. Whatever it was that you two did, it was what you two did. This is the chicken and the egg conversation because, after a while, neither of you could identify "who started it." It was simply the dance you danced during your marriage.

When you separate and divorce, the dance should change. You are no longer interacting over the minutia of day-to-day living and the old patterns do not effectively resolve the larger issues. But your ex-spouse's behavior will not change with a request from you. You must manage the change by positively and negatively reinforcing behavior. In doing so, however, keep in mind you may not be able to accurately predict how your ex-spouse will respond. Just as the divorce has changed you, it has changed them, too. That is not to say your ex-spouse's basic character has changed, but it does mean you do not have the same lens to predict their behavior as you once had while living together.

Because you are no longer sharing a home, you lack a certain level of intimacy. Where once when hour ex-spouse came in the door you could see they had a difficult day at work, now you no longer know what happened during their day. Now, how they respond to you may be more about what happened with their boss than it is about you, but you do not know that. Because you no longer share a life, you simply do not know the things that happen that impact your ex-spouse. Any tool you select, therefore, must be chosen based on the most recent data. While strategizing and anticipating your ex-spouse's likely response to any given situation, remember to consider recent changes in behavior and adjust accordingly.

At the same time, your ex-spouse believes they know you. They certainly know how to push your buttons. This is because they know your values, something that is not likely to change significantly over time, and therefore they intuitively understand what will drive you over the edge. By modifying your responses to their attempted triggers, you teach them that you are no longer predictable. Instead of responding the same way – always in anger, for example – dance a new dance. Dance the unpredictability dance. By consciously becoming unpredictable, you loosen your ex-spouse's grip on you.

Jeremy's ex-wife continued abusing him long after their divorce. Jeremy was a soft-spoken and generous man who had done his best to make her happy. She had grown accustomed to his acquiescence and continued making unreasonable demands from him. She wrote scathing emails belittling him for not doing as he was told. For a while, he continued trying to appease her, but eventually he began changing his demeanor when he interacted with her. At times, he remained calm, but at other times he began to shout and insult. Occasionally, he pulled off the road while driving home from work to call and scream at her. Eventually, Jeremy's ex-wife learned not to take his compliance for granted. When she wanted something, she began to ask, not demand. Because she no longer knew what to expect from him, she became more cautious and polite in her communication and ultimately there was less negative interaction between them.

There is power in being unpredictable. By mindfully choosing when to be compliant and calm, and when to unleash your inner beast, you will teach your ex-spouse not to be complacent towards you.

THE "CONSISTENCY" TRAP

Legal and mental health professionals speak of the importance of consistency for children's development. I agree; however, I have seen parents try to control their ex-spouses by demanding consistency. That is, one parent would impose a rule in their house and then demand the same rule be imposed in their former spouse's house. Without consensus, this is unfair. Robyn, for example, frequently contacted her ex-husband and demanded that he punish the children because they misbehaved in her house. She insisted he deprive them of the television or computer because his failure to do so would send an inconsistent message and confuse the children. The problem is that Robyn's ex-husband did not always agree with her rules or her punishments.

When parents are married, they usually discuss both the crime and the punishment. There is consensus. When Robyn punished her child for an infraction of her household rule, her ex-husband had no say in either the making of the rule or the imposition of the punishment. His knowledge of the situation was entirely filtered through Robyn. In this situation, Robyn's ex-husband believed she was too harsh and inflexible. Robyn is very rule-driven. Thus, he was not inclined to agree with her.

The problem for Robyn's ex-husband and others is that he cannot refuse simply because he dislikes her. On the other hand, he should not capitulate simply because she argues that consistency is important. He must judge each situation individually. The reality is that the children *do* live in two separate homes now that their parents are divorced, and they will have to adjust to two sets of rules. It is not detrimental to them. In school, they must adjust to each teacher's different rules as well. They will have to learn to adjust to different bosses in the workplace, too. Hopefully, both parents have consistently taught the basic rules of respect and responsibility, but when and how a child cleans their bedroom or does their homework need not be entirely consistent.

Be mindful, however, that *respect* does mean different things to different people. A borderline-personality individual will interpret respect as "following their rules." Such a parent will punish their children for being disrespectful if they break the rules, even if the rules change inconsistently or if they are illogical. Heather refused to allow her 16-year-old son to drive her car unless he signed a contract agreeing to pay both the cost of repair should he get into an accident *and* the monthly increase in her insurance costs resulting from that accident. Her son thought this *rule* was too strict. He was willing to pay for the car repairs, but not her insurance because he understood that her insurance premiums were not based solely on *his* driving record but on other factors as well, such as the distance she drove to work. He also thought that paying for the damage to the car if the accident was not his fault but was caused by another driver was unfair. Was he being disrespectful by refusing her conditions? Heather thought so. Her ex-husband, the boy's father, disagreed. He thought the boy's arguments were sound and he believed that the 16-year-old demonstrated respect (and good critical-thinking skills) by listening and considering his mother's concerns and by making his best efforts to drive safely. Heather was so uncompromising that she prohibited her son from driving at her house because he disrespected her by refusing to abide by her rules. The result was that her son resented her unreasonableness and spent more time with his father, who allowed him to drive the car to school and work. Heather's notion of *respect* was vastly different from her ex-husband's.

Be aware of parents who exploit the concept of consistency to further their own ends. If your ex-spouse speaks of co-parenting and working together for the sake of the children, study their actions. Make certain that you are part of the dialogue. If communication is only one way and you are not being heard, then the words are probably a smokescreen to distract you from your ex-spouse's true purpose: to remain engaged in your life. I like the brick wall test. If you get as much feedback from your ex-spouse as you do from speaking to a brick wall, then you might as well talk to the wall and forget about conversing with your ex.

STAY OFF THE EMOTIONAL-ROLLER COASTER

It is difficult to stand aside and watch your family be together without you. People sometimes imagine their children and ex-spouse as if they were living in a Hallmark or Lifetime movie. They envision everyone laughing and loving while they are excluded, outside, and alone. For personality-disordered people suffering from poor coping and adjustment skills, these mental images can be devastating. That is one reason they try so hard to remain engaged in the lives of their ex-spouses. They cannot accept the perceived rejection.

Because these individuals lack self-awareness, they often fail to grasp the consequences of their actions. They interpret your behavior as if you acted in a vacuum, failing to comprehend that you had, in fact, reacted to them. It is as if each moment in their life is disconnected from the previous moment. They are victimized by countless enemies and fail to understand why the world is so cruel. That may even have been part of the reason you married – because you are an inherit rescuer. But because this person is a black-and-white thinker, you no longer are their rescuer; now you are the enemy. Now your disordered ex-spouse metaphorically stands outside your door, hurt and angry that you have barred their entrance.

They will construct reasons, real or imagined, to regain admission to your life. Just after Sarah remarried, her ex-husband and her new husband's ex-wife, Madison, had a birthday celebration for *Sarah's* child. This was on a weekend when both ex-spouses had parenting time and Sarah and her new husband were enjoying some rare time alone together. Neither Sarah nor her new husband were invited to this party, yet the ex-spouses told the children they were helping the new stepsiblings bond. Later, it was challenging to explain the distortion of this reality to them. The children were now related through Sarah and her new husband, *not* through Sarah's ex-husband and Madison.

This surreal experience illustrates the lengths to which Sarah's ex-husband went to remain engaged in her life. He created a situation he knew would anger her. Sarah was smart, though. She did not react. Had she sent him an email complaining about what he and Madison had done, he would have been rewarded. He would have known for certain that he had gotten under her skin. Instead, Sarah was a blank page with him, although she did explain the absurdity of the event to the children. The children understood that had they *really* been "one big happy extended family," Sarah and her new husband would have been invited to the party as well.

The following year, Madison sent balloons to Sarah's son to celebrate his birthday. The week before, however, she had refused to allow her children to remain with Sarah and their father for an extra two hours to celebrate that same birthday with Sarah's family (her parents and brother) who could only arrive later due to a scheduling conflict. Madison refused for no other reason than she *could* say "no." The children did not have school the next day, or any other activities that would require them to wake up early. For Madison, it was all about control.

From a distance, both events may seem innocuous. A children's party. A balloon bouquet. But the instigator of these events, your ex-spouse, is inconsistent. One minute they are refusing you time to celebrate and the next minute they are hosting a party. One minute they grant you additional time with your child and the next minute they deny you. This inconsistent behavior reflects your ex-spouse's internal chaos. Your ex-spouse is on an emotional roller- coaster. You should not allow yourself to ride along. If you find yourself happy one day because they were nice to you and devastated the next because they were cruel, then you are on a coaster that they are driving. Get off.

It is difficult not to let your former spouse's behavior affect you. They can appear rational and may even succeed at eliciting your sympathy. At one time, you saw the world through their eyes. You nurtured them because they were victimized, and you are a rescuer.

But your personality disordered ex-spouse lives from crisis to crisis, from one person having wronged them to the next. You do not need to live in that world any longer. You do not need to be their enemy one minute and their ally the next. Maintain your boundaries and manage situations to the best of your ability without including them. Sarah and her husband spoke directly to their children about the party and the balloons. They explained the inconsistencies in their other parent's behavior. They did not disparage the other parents. They did not use viscous names or distorted facts. The facts spoke for themselves. Sarah's stepdaughter already knew she had been prohibited from staying for the party. Her father and Sarah simply helped her draw the connection between two contrary acts. In that way, they hoped that when Madison made other inconsistent decisions – which they knew would happen – the children would be less confused. The children would trust their gut when it told them that things did not make sense, and they would be less likely to blame themselves. Sarah and her husband were teaching their children to stay off their personality-disordered parent's emotional roller-coaster, too.

PARENTING YOURSELF DURING THIS EMOTIONAL TRANSITION

Divorce is a major life transition, and transitions always involve loss. You are losing money. You are losing financial stability. You may lose your home, your neighborhood, and even your community should you be forced to move far away. You are losing your position in your society as part of a couple. Everyone knows it is more difficult to socialize as a single person when all your friends are coupled off. But, most important, you are losing your expectations that you and your chosen partner in life would marry, build a family, and live happily ever after. You are losing that fantasy of family.

For involved parents, one of the biggest losses in a divorce is the loss of connection with your children. The changing relationship with your children that results from your divorce will be your most permanent and enduring loss. Unless your children's other parent has completely relinquished physical and legal custody, you will lose time with your children. Even if the other parent has visitation for only two hours a week, there now will be two hours a week when the law prohibits you from seeing your children.

You will also lose some control over your children. When your children are with their other parent, you can no longer make decisions about their life. You cannot control when they go to bed, or if they finish their homework, or what they eat for dinner. You cannot control whether your ex-spouse introduces your children to their newest romantic relationship, or whether they let your child get a tattoo. Finally, even if you are close, your children will now have experiences with their other parent that do not include you. Their other parent might take them scuba diving or skiing, something you cannot or chose not to do. This is an experience you cannot share with your children, and they probably will choose not to share with you. It is different from your children being out with a friend and coming home to tell you all about it. They will not tell you what happened at their other parent's house. It is none of your business.

What hurts more, though, is that they may want to be with their other parent even though you think their other parent is *Satan Personified*. Children are hard wired to want the love and approval of their parents and will suffer a lot to get it. Now, even if you despise their other parent, they do not. Recognize that during and after your divorce your children's interests and needs will become different from yours or, at the very least, different from what you think they should be. And this is a big loss to a parent.

All of these loses need to be acknowledged and mourned. If there was ever a time for therapy, this is it. Like your children, you will cycle through your grief, anger, and fear, along with some feelings of relief and hope. Sometimes you will feel all these emotions at the same time. You are likely to suffer from depression and anxiety. High-conflict divorces are not over for up to five years after the final judgment is signed by the judge. Living with heightened emotions for prolonged periods of time can be damaging. Therapy will help you process those feelings and the events that generated them. It will help you come to terms with your high-conflict divorce.

Still, there are ways to help yourself without therapy. Never forget that this period of your life *will* pass. You will have a future life that does not include your ex-spouse. You just have to hold out. In the meantime, practice the "Bill Clinton." Regardless of what you think of the former president, he was known for his ability to compart-mentalize. It is commonly known that one of the keys to his success was his ability to focus on one thing at a time. It is a great skill, but to make it work during this time of stress, allow yourself time to feel, too. To help yourself focus, promise yourself you will have time later in the day to *feel*.

Acknowledge what you are leaving behind. Learn to identify and express your feelings. While it is normal to try to push away feelings of fear and anxiety, you will move through them more quickly if you acknowledge them. These feelings will have less power over you if you face them and express them. If your day is filled with tasks, then fill your nights with emotions. Take time to cry. Take time to scream and yell (out of hearing range of your children, of course).

Acknowledge your feelings by writing them down or talking about them with trusted friends and family members. If you are feeling overwhelmed during the day, give yourself a time-out. Take a coffee break, a walk, or a run. You will not do yourself or anyone any good if you cannot think straight. The key is to honor your feelings and your need to think clearly. Make certain each day allows time for both.

For some, the ability to separate thoughts and emotions seems monumentally difficult, but it is doable. The key is to be mindful of yourself. Mindfulness skills teach that there are three primary states of mind: (1) the reasonable mind that approaches the world from an intellectual point of view; (2) the emotional mind; and (3) the wise mind, which integrates both. Balance your emotional and reasonable minds by focusing on the present moment. Mentally slam the door on everything else. Concentrate in small bursts and you are more likely to be able to succeed at your task. Stare foggily at a lengthy "to do" list and you are not likely to move forward. If you are facing a task and unable to concentrate, then be mindful and acknowledge your difficulty. Use your "wise mind" and allow yourself a "time out" to feel. Then use your rational mind to rally for 10 or 15 minutes of concentrated effort. The 30 minutes you spent feeling and thinking were far more productive than the 30 minutes you would have spent staring blankly at your project.

Second, always strive to face your reality. Differentiate between "wants" and "shoulds." It is critical to stop yourself from "expecting" your ex-spouse to behave in a certain way. Do not fall into the trap of thinking "they should do this" for their children. You have those thoughts because you *want* your ex-spouse to be the parent you expected (and hoped for) when you first married. But those thoughts will only lead to disappointment. Be mindful so that when they creep into your conscious you can dismiss them. Exchange them for the thought "they are likely to do this." This will help you effectively strategize your own interactions. If you are having difficulty letting go of the disappointment that your ex-spouse is not behaving as they "should," then during your "feeling" time allow yourself to mourn the fantasy of what you thought they were and what you wanted them to be.

Accept that the fundamental nature of reality is change. Mourn your losses. You have many, and they should be honored. But do not expend energy railing against the fact that your life is not static. No life is. No one leads a charmed life. Continue reminding yourself that "this too shall pass." Everything changes and so, too, will this difficult stage of your life.

Expect to feel uncomfortable. A time of transition is confusing and disorienting. It is normal to feel insecure and anxious. These feelings are part of the process, and they, too, will pass. Take one step at a time. It is understandable to feel like your life has become unmanageable. To regain a sense of power, find one small thing you can control right now. Then break it down into small, specific, concrete steps. Write them down and post them on your computer monitor or bathroom mirror. Cross off each step as you accomplish it. Applaud yourself for what you have accomplished each day.

Take care of yourself. Transitions are incredibly stressful and if you do not feel well enough to participate in your normal activities, then find something fun to do for yourself each day. Get plenty of rest, exercise, and eat well. But try to keep some things consistent. This will help normalize your emotions during this difficult transition.

Build your support system. Seek the support of friends and family members, especially those who accept you without judging, and who encourage you to express your true feelings. A time of transition is also an excellent time to seek the support of a mental health professional.

Accept that you may never completely understand what has happened to you and why. You will never "get into your ex-spouse's head" or make them "see the light." This makes most of us extremely uncomfortable. We like closure but in high-conflict divorces that rarely happens. Know your discomfort and confusion will pass, and clarity will return. In the interim, honor the fact that you are suffering many major losses in your life. Take time to mourn. But, like everything else, mourn smart. Compartmentalize the pain and allow yourself time to feel it. But be certain you do have that *Pity Party* because feelings are like water surging beyond the dam. They will eventually bust through unless you release them, slowly and steadily.

THE ONE-, THREE-, AND FIVE-YEAR PLAN

At the same time your life is deconstructing, you must begin reconstructing as well. Your life will go on and, as you divide property and debt and determine custody of your children, you will need to consider what your life will look like going forward. Life transitions offer you the chance to explore what your ideal life might look like. When things are in disarray, you can reflect on the hopes and dreams you once had but had forgotten.

Identify your values and life goals. Knowing who you are and what you want from life may help you see the divorce as another life challenge. If you always wanted to go back to school or change careers, now might be the time to do it. This is because you now have an opportunity to ask the court to have your ex-spouse help fund it. Judges appreciate people who are trying to improve their situation, and if you argue you need financial assistance you may convince that judge to order your ex-spouse to do what they ordinarily would have refused to do.

Spend some time considering where you would like to see yourself in five years' time. Where will you live? What will you be doing professionally? Do you see yourself married again? Once you have identified that five-year goal, consider where you need to be in three years to be three-fifths of the way to your long-term goal. Will you be in a new home? Will you be in a new job? Will you be an Internet Dating-Site-Survivor? Now move your sights forward to a year from the day your divorce is finalized. What do you need to be doing to reach your goals at that three-year mark? How much money will you need to save? Can you live frugally for three years so you can buy a bigger house then instead of compromising now? If you are receiving support, can you save some of that money and live only on what you earn, so you have a bigger down payment in three years? These are the questions to begin thinking about during this transition period. By planning for your future, you will help yourself transition from this unpleasant present.

CHAPTER ELEVEN:

I t is essential to have a good filing system in a high-conflict divorce. Much of your correspondence with your attorney, including the exchange of draft documents, will be via email. It is your choice to keep documents on your computer or printed out, or both, but in either case, you must maintain a good filing system. Have plenty of well-labeled files. Remember those subpoenas to Allen's ex-wife's husband? She had claimed in a prior action that she owned a business jointly with her new husband. If Allen had not remembered that statement and been able to produce the document it was written on, he would not have had a basis for filing the subpoenas. A good filing system, including a good labeling system, is critical in your high-conflict divorce. You will need to access and re-access documents from prior legal actions to support current legal actions.

You want to have three sets of files: one for court documents, one for emails and one for billing.

Court Documents: Every time you go to court you are there because either you or your former spouse has filed a motion. Each motion is a mini lawsuit. Create a separate file for each suit. Within each file, have a section for pleadings (the legal documents filed in court), a section for correspondence with your attorney and a section for evidence. The pleading file will be the most difficult to maintain because you and your attorney will trade drafts of pleadings before the final draft is filed. It is your choice whether to keep or dispose of the initial drafts but be certain to keep the final draft.

The evidence section of this file may include emails from your ex-spouse. I recommend that you keep *copies* of the emails from your ex-spouse within each lawsuit file and keep the original in your email file. That is because one email may be needed as evidence in different lawsuits, and you may lose an email if the sole copy is stored away in an earlier lawsuit file.

Email: Because the conflict in high-conflict divorces lasts for years, you may want to organize emails from your ex-spouse by year or topic. Or both. Sometimes you will exchange emails for a week or two about a specific topic, such as whether Johnny needs braces. You may want to keep copies of those emails in a folder labeled "2014" or "Braces." In either case, you will want *copies* of those emails as evidence for the motion you file asking for an order requiring the other parent to pay for the braces. Do not store the only copy of the email in the "Motion for Braces" file you are preparing. Do keep a copy in a separate file labeled "Braces" or "2014" (or whatever year it is). There is a good chance you will need those emails for another completely unrelated situation. Perhaps Johnny's younger sister, Jill, will need braces, too, and you will be back in court in another two years fighting the same battle. Or, more likely, your ex-spouse will testify in court and in their own affidavit that they *always* pay for their children and, therefore, your current lawsuit against them is frivolous. How are you going to refute that if you do not have evidence they are lying? It would be your word against theirs. But if you have proof – if you have their email from three years ago evidencing their refusal to pay for Johnny's braces –

Yes, you waste a lot of paper in high-conflict divorces, but it is better to have copies when and where you need them than to waste hours of time and emotional energy searching for the documents you need.

Bills: If your former spouse refuses to pay their share of your child's expenses, it may be easier on you to bill them monthly, rather than as the bills arise. Every time you bill your former spouse, store it in a separate file specifically designated for that year or quarter-year. Send them a copy of the bills for that month, along with an invoice outlining the reason for the bill, the total cost, and their percentage. Include at the end the unpaid balance from the previous month. Then keep a copy of each packet that includes the bills, the invoice, and the cover letter. In that way, when you sue them for failing to pay, you can simply gather all your packets, make a copy for the court, and everything is already organized for you.

CHAPTER TWELVE:

The end result of the divorce legal proceeding is an order – or set of orders – establishing custody and visitation, dividing property and debt, and allocating income for child and spousal support. There is always *buyer's remorse*. A successful mediation is defined as both parties having given up something to achieve resolution. Neither party gets everything they want. If you went to trial, the judge would not give you everything you wanted either. The judge will focus on the big picture, garnering sufficient facts to determine whether they should order something other than a 50-50 split. They will not, for example, spend a great deal of time determining if Friday parenting time should start at 3 p.m. or 3:30 p.m. To them, the difference is miniscule. To you and your children, however, the difference may be paramount, especially because these are the details that add fuel to your high-conflict divorce. You may continue fighting for that 30 minute long after the divorce is finalized.

Sometimes couples reach agreement "on the courthouse steps" just before the trial is set to start. While this saves money – the cost of the trial itself – it may result in greater expense later, as it is difficult to negotiate the many details required to draft a final judgment in a high-conflict divorce. Again, larger issues will be resolved, but not the details.

Mary and her ex-husband agreed that each would keep their own car and remove the other from the title and loan. No time frame for completing this was established. The result was that Mary's ex-husband continued delaying removing her name from the loan and stopped making payments. The creditor pursued Mary for payment and she had to go to court and ask the judge to force him to remove her name from the loan. He argued that he could not do it for a variety of reasons and asked for more time, which the judge gave him. Had Mary's order required him to complete the task within a specified period, her ex-husband would have made the same argument, but he would have less credibility. That is because he would now be directly defying a court order, which angers the judge. The focus of the discussion would not be on why he could not complete the task within a reasonable time, but why he could not complete the task in the time he had agreed to. It is a subtle difference, but one that undermines his credibility and may result in a ruling that is more favorable to Mary. It is not an issue Mary could have predicted and preempted in a judgment of divorce that was drafted an hour before her trial was scheduled to start.

Once an agreement is reached or the trial judge rules, a Judgment of Divorce (JOD) is entered. This is the court order granting your divorce and outlining your post-judgment rights. Some jurisdictions include everything in a single document: property settlements, spousal support, custody, and child support. Others provide you with a collection of separate orders. *Keep your orders readily available.* Make copies and preserve the originals in a safe place. The copies should be easily accessible. You will need to refer to them whenever conflicts arise and, in high-conflict cases, post-judgment conflicts arise frequently. It is essential to always maintain good records. After the JOD is entered, continue recording when your ex-spouse was late or missed parenting time. Record if your children return home exhausted, starving, and dirty. This provides your evidence that, despite all claims to the contrary, your ex-spouse is not the parent they claim to be. At some point, you may accumulate sufficient evidence to prove to the court that the plan is not working.

It is difficult to modify a JOD on the grounds that you did not fully understand what you were signing. That is because in most courts, before the judge signs the final orders, the parties are asked to testify under oath that they have read the proposed final orders. Once they have read them and testified, they are charged with full knowledge. This makes it difficult to return later and say, "I didn't know" or "I didn't understand." You may appeal the JOD, but if you and your ex-spouse testified under oath that you agree with its terms, you will not have any grounds. Changing your mind after the fact is challenging at best. Appealing the JOD after a trial requires you to allege that the judge made an error of law. If you win the appeal, what you gain is another long and costly trial.

PARENTING AFTER DIVORCE IN HIGH-CONFLICT CASES

Because it is widely believed that children should have ongoing relationship with both parents, co-parenting is considered the ideal post-divorce parenting arrangement. When divorced parents co-parent, they work cooperatively to provide for their children. To be workable, the ex-spouses/parents must mutually respect and support one another. They must communicate regularly. They must be able to share major medical and education decisions as well as decisions about extracurricular activities, summer camp programs, and all the other activities children regularly participate in. Studies consistently evidence that when divorced parents interact with one another in non-hostile ways, children's recovery is expedited. Co-parent cooperation involves regular communication and coordinating consistent practices.

Having both parents involved in children's lives post-divorce is an ideal, but the reality is that co-parenting couples are vulnerable to conflict. When two parents from different households are both engaged in managing a single child, it is natural there will be disagreements, even if the divorce was not high conflict. After Matt and Anne divorced, they went to therapy together to establish protocols for co-parenting. Several sessions with the therapist included the children. Matt purchased a home near Anne so the children could remain in their school district. At first, the family followed the parenting plan, which was week on-week off. But neither parent strictly adhered to the schedule. If a child wanted to be at Matt's house on Tuesday, both parents were agreeable. On holidays, Matt's and Anne's extended family all celebrated together. Similarly, Serena and her new husband celebrated Christmas with both sets of children (his and hers), including both ex-spouses and both of their new spouses. They jokingly referred to the event as the "X-Mass." Still, there were issues that had to be resolved, such as who would pay for what activity and which high school the children would attend.

Co-parenting is workable, but not in high-conflict cases. For these couples, the same problems they faced during the marriage and divorce – disrespect and inability to cooperate – plague them after the divorce. High-conflict parents remain highly conflicted and rarely transform into cooperative parents. The default option for resolving day-to-day issues is litigation. The conflicts will be over small issues such as ambiguities in the parenting plan and larger issues such as chronically unworkable schedules. If you litigate frequently, there is a chance the judge will decide you and your ex-spouse are unable to co-parent.

George was so hostile and volatile that despite his efforts for joint legal custody, he could not restrain himself. Emails to his wife were replete with insults, calling her "bitch" and "whore." Even in court, he could not stop himself from shouting invectives. George lost legal custody. If a parent demonstrates that they are incapable of co-parenting, the judge may give the other parent sole legal and/or physical custody.

Co-parenting is not appropriate if there is a risk of ongoing violence. The abusive ex-spouse will sacrifice the children by using them as weapons, forcing the other parent to relent. They will use visitation to remain in contact with their ex-spouse and to preserve their abusive hold.

If parents cannot co-parent, some courts require them to attend parent education courses, but these have dubious results. Although such programs have enjoyed relative success with divorces that are not high-conflict, the efficacy of education programs targeting high-conflict parents has not been evaluated. One of the challenges facing such programs is that they are often based on the presumption that people are rational and will act in their children's best interests. In high-conflict cases, that is not always the case. Disordered parents *will* sacrifice their children to achieve their goals. After years of post-judgment litigation, a judge ordered Kyrsten and her ex-husband to attend an education program geared at high-conflict couples. Kyrsten and her ex-husband were each told to select one issue of paramount importance and "work it out." The objective was to demonstrate that if they could resolve one issue, they could resolve others. The problem was that Kyrsten refused to even consider her ex-husband's issue, which was the *right of first refusal* (the right to parenting time instead of having the children watched by a babysitter when Kyrsten went out). After eight weeks, the facilitators of the program gave up. No agreement was reached. What the court personnel did not understand was Kyrsten's resilience, the underlying motives behind her refusal to cooperate, and that she was willing to sacrifice the children (have them watched by a babysitter and not their dad) rather than submit to the will of her ex-husband. Nor did they understand that even had an agreement been reached, no "bank account" would have been created. The disordered parent reflexively rewrites history and would not remember this moment of cooperation. The only thing the experience taught Kyrsten was that if she continued to litigate, the court could demand eight weeks of her time. She took the battle outside the courthouse and the conflict continued.

PARENTAL ALIENATION

Psychiatrist Richard Gardner first coined the term **parental alienation** in 1985. It is generally defined as behaviors, conscious or unconscious, designed to damage the relationship between a child and the targeted parent. Parental alienation results in the child adopting unreasonable negative feelings and beliefs towards a parent without any basis. The child's anger, hatred or rejection is inconsistent with that child's experience with the parent.

A child's unsubstantiated hatred of the *targeted parent* is believed to be a result of the other parent's brainwashing. The child is indoctrinated into believing that the targeted parent is dangerous, malicious and does not love the child. When asked, however, the child cannot produce any facts to substantiate his perspective.

Parental alienation has engendered widespread debate regarding its validity. Many criticize the lack of empirical data. Also noteworthy is the fact that it was not included in the Diagnostic and Statistical Manual of Mental Disorders–5, which was released in 2013. Nonetheless, abusive parents commonly sabotage their ex-spouse's relationship with the children and often blame that parent. Worse, they portray themselves as innocent and the other parent as mentally unstable. The abusive ex-spouse often sets up their ex-spouse, so they appear to be the abuser. They do this by deliberately provoking them until they respond with a physical or verbal attack. The alienating parent then highlights their actions as evidence of the *other parent's* ongoing antagonism – anything to validate themselves in front of their children and the court as stable and secure.

Regardless of whether parental alienation is an actual syndrome, your ex-spouse may employ one or more of these devastating tactics to alienate you from your children:

- ❖ Accusing the targeted parent of molesting a child.
- ❖ Creating false memories for the child such as "When you were an infant your dad beat you."

- ❖ Telling a child to accuse the targeted parent of having sex with them.
- ❖ Forcing a child to testify in court against the targeted parent.
- ❖ Telling the child that the targeted parent plans to kill or kidnap them.
- ❖ Making the child feel guilty about their relationship with the targeted parent by telling them they will be lonely without the child, and that they will miss the child when they are with the targeted parent.
- ❖ Telling the child that they will not be loved unless they live with this parent.
- ❖ Withdrawing love if the child has fun with the targeted parent.
- ❖ Expressing anger if the child speaks to the targeted parent.
- ❖ Denying visitation or interfering with the targeted parent's right to participate in children's activities.
- ❖ Forcing the child to choose between spending parenting time with the targeted parent and rejecting the alienating parent's fun activity.
- ❖ Letting the child decide whether to visit the targeted parent in contravention of court orders.
- ❖ Making subliminal suggestions such as "your dad isn't fun" or "your dad didn't call you today, did he?"
- ❖ Telling the child to draft an email saying they do not want to see the targeted parent or telling the child to hang up when the targeted parent calls.
- ❖ Turning off the phone, changing the phone number, blocking calls, snatching the phone from the child, or requiring that

telephone contact with the targeted parent only be through the alienating parent's cell phone.

❖ Telling the child that they cannot talk to the targeted parent while they are at the alienating parent's house.

❖ Forbidding the child to acknowledge the targeted parent when they see each other in public.

❖ Having the child spy on the targeted parent and report back on everything that goes on in the targeted parent's house.

❖ Prohibiting the targeted parent from giving the child gifts by returning them, misplacing them, or breaking them.

❖ Telling the child that the gifts are because the targeted parent is trying to buy their love.

❖ Destroying all photos of the targeted parent and demanding that the child remove the targeted parent from the family tree school assignment.

❖ Telling the child to call the alienating parent's significant other "mom" or "dad.

❖ Refusing to provide the targeted parent with information from the school, doctors, and social activities.

❖ Badmouthing the targeted parent to friends, teachers, and doctors.

❖ Cutting ties with anyone that might support the targeted parent.

The list is lengthy and not comprehensive. Abusive ex-spouses are clever and the ways to instigate negativity are endless. But there are ways to combat the impact of your ex-spouse's efforts.

The most fundamental change must be accepting that you and your ex-spouse live two separate lives and co-parenting is not, in the foreseeable future, a possibility. You must shift your paradigm to minimize all reliance on your ex-spouse. The parent who complained that his ex-spouse hid or destroyed his gifts to his children had no reason to give the gifts to her. They should have been given directly to the children during *his* parenting time. The parent who complained that his ex-wife refused to tell him his children's cell phone numbers should never have relied on her to facilitate his communication with his children. He should have purchased cell phones for them and if they must carry around two, so be it. Nor should any parent complain that their ex-spouse refused to give them information about school events or doctor appointments. These parents should be establishing mechanisms to access the information directly from the source. If a parent has legal custody (even if shared with an ex-spouse) then that parent has legal access to school and medical records. The fundamental flaw is in the *targeted parent's* continued reliance on their ex-spouse to facilitate their relationship with their children after the divorce. This *grants* the alienating parent the power to be a gatekeeper.

The paradigm *must* shift in high-conflict divorces. Communication is toxic and therefore is to be avoided as much as possible. Instead of co-parenting, you and your ex-spouse must **parallel parent**.

PARALLEL PARENTING

In parallel parenting, communication between the parents is extremely limited, thereby reducing opportunities for conflict. Communication should only be through email and only about logistical issues involving both parents. If Zach has a baseball game that is on his mother's time, his father should *not* ask her when and where the game is. Zach's father should acquire that information independently and attend the game regardless of whether his ex-wife wants him there or not. He should make certain Zach knows that he is there cheering for him. If, however, the game begins on Zach's mother's time and ends on his father's time, Zach's father should send the mother a short email confirming that he will pick Zach up directly from the game and that she should please make certain Zach has everything he needs such as clothing and schoolbooks. There should be no further discussion.

Verbal communication between the parents should not occur unless there is a real emergency. There should never be telephone or texting about issues such as grades or problems with friends at school. Those should be addressed directly with the child. Face-to-face communication should be minimized as well. A polite "hello" as parents pass one another at an event will suffice. But always be polite, especially in public, where others can observe and report on your behavior.

Soon after his divorce was finalized, Jerome asked his ex-wife to meet to discuss setting up college accounts for their children. Alarmed at the prospect of co-owning an account with her ex-husband, she declined. As they were leaving the coffee shop, she asked if he would open his own account for the children and he said no. He would not do it without her participation. Clearly then, his invitation to co-parent by co-owning a college account was Jerome's attempt to remain involved in his ex-wife's life. It had nothing to do with the children. Parallel parenting reduces the opportunity for an abusive parent to exploit visitation and decision making as a way of perpetuating the abuse. It reduces tensions and attempts at alienation. The less contact the parents have with one another, the less likely they are to antagonize each other. Each parent is responsible for the day-to-day needs of the children during their parenting time. Each parent provides for their children. Thus, clothing and toys are not transported between houses. The only property that should be transported from mother's house to father's house are school materials and extracurricular supplies (musical instruments, baseball uniforms, etc.).

To effectively parallel parent, both parents must accept that neither may affect the children's lives while they are with the other parent. They have no say and may not influence the actions of the other parent while the children are in the other parent's care. There is no expectation of flexibility or negotiation. A parent does not plan activities for the children during the other parent's time.

Parallel parenting has been criticized for requiring the children to live two distinct lives, with two sets of rules and expectations. There is no consistency. But the reduction in conflict outweighs this condemnation. And consistency is a myth. In school, children must sit in different classrooms with different teachers who have different teaching styles and different rules. When they begin working, they will have to learn to accommodate different bosses with different management styles. Even teenagers working at a McDonald's restaurant may have two different shift managers with different expectations and communication styles. To function in this world, we all need to adapt. Children are resilient, but it is better for them to learn adaptation skills than to continue living in a world where their parents are constantly fighting.

Another benefit to parallel parenting is that it exposes children to alternative values and living styles. If their mother is rule-driven and inflexible, for example, and their father is adaptable, the children learn that there is more than one way of doing things. Suppose the parents did not divorce and the children were raised in a house with multiple rules and harsh punishments for breaking them. Suppose their mother created this culture and their father accepted it to keep the peace. The children would grow up believing that rules are inflexible and breaking them is painful. They will go out into the world holding that paradigm and may be shocked to learn that others do not share it. How will they respond? They may become judgmental and hostile to those who "flaunt" the rules. They may be incapable of seeing that some rules are bad, such as a rule that prohibits employees from taking a bathroom break until their three-hour shift is over. They may alienate others with their inflexibility.

If, on the other hand, the children are exposed to another household where rules are given less weight, they learn that there are diverse ways of functioning in the world. This is not a terrible thing. Better still if their other parent discusses their views and asks about theirs. This opens a dialogue that acknowledges the reality of the children's lifestyle, respects them enough to hear how they feel and what challenges they face, and ultimately builds relationship bonds.

Hostile parents trying to co-parent is like trying to shove the proverbial square peg into a round hole. It simply will not work. Better to acknowledge that and stop the futile effort than to continue trying to cooperate. That strategy will only lead to failure.

THE CHOSEN CHILD

When talking with your children, recognize that each may have different experiences and relationships with their other parent. Studies have found that not all children are equally affected by *parental alienation* strategies. Parents do treat their children differently. This has to do with the child's personality and temperament, the child's role in the family system, the child's relationship with other members of the family, and the parent's own personality and expectations of his or her children.

There is also the **chosen child** effect. A disordered parent often selects a child as special. This may be a conscious or unconscious choice, but the result is that the parent connects to the **chosen child** in a way that differs from their connection to their other offspring. The chosen child is special because they are perceived as smarter, better looking, funnier etc. than the other children. This phenomenon is particularly apparent with people suffering from narcissistic personality disorder. The narcissistic parent believes that the chosen child "is just like me."

When the chosen child is young, their special status may award them gifts or better treatment than the other children receive. As they child ages, however, this child is the most likely to be abused. Why might the "chosen" child be abused? A narcissist parent identifies with this child. They see in this child everything they believe themself to be. To the narcissistic parent, their younger child reflects the **Public Persona** that the narcissist believes is their true self. The narcissist then expects this chosen child to behave as the narcissist believes they would behave. The narcissist parent expects the chosen child to do their bidding, the same as they expect their arm to move on command. But the child is an independent person and may or may not do what the parent expects. This refusal to comply can enrage a narcissist parent who may then physically or emotionally abuse the child. The narcissist parent both adores and despises their chosen child. They adore the fantasy and despise the reality. Their relationship is a cycle of "I love you" and "I hate you."

This child will grow up doubting themselves and their ability to comprehend the world. As a young child, they witnessed the public, friends, and neighbors, responding to their narcissistic parent's charm, accepting the **Public Persona** as real. But behind closed doors this child is exposed to their narcissist parent's rage and ridicule. How can this young child understand that their parent has two personalities? If other people think their parent is nice, then they, too, should believe their parent is nice, and therefore their fear or anger must be wrong. The problem, the child concludes, must be with "me."

As this confused young child grows into adolescence, where it is developmentally appropriate for them to begin questioning their parent's rules and values, the narcissistic parent's anger grows even stronger. While having been raised not to believe in themself, this adolescent child fights harder to find their own identity. They struggle to separate from the parent who sees them as "just like me." The "I love you/I hate you" cycle becomes weighted towards the anger and hate as the narcissist parent fights to retain control over both the child and the fantasy. It is then that the chosen child is most at risk for abuse, while the other children, disregarded, remain safe.

Unless your attorney and judge have degrees in mental health, they are unlikely to accept that a parent may only abuse one of several children or that only one child is the target of that parent's alienation efforts. Therefore, unless your child is in physical danger, the legal system is not the best forum for resolving issues of parental emotional abuse or alienation. To negate these effects, you must actively build your relationship with your children.

BUILDING YOUR RELATIONSHIP WITH YOUR CHILD

You can remain involved in your children's lives by being involved in their activities and having relationships with the people who touch their world. Do not rely on the other parent to give you information about doctor appointments or issues at school. That enables the other parent to function as a gatekeeper. Establish your own relationships with your child's coaches, teachers, and healthcare providers. Let these people know that if there is an issue, they should contact you directly.

Coach their teams. Volunteer at school. Attend every practice and every game. Be the parent who hosts the end-of-the-season dinner. Go to school open houses and parent-teacher conferences. Most schools now have online access to children's grades. Monitor your children's grades and help them with their homework and projects when they are with you. Larry helped his son with his English papers by having him email them from his mother's house. Larry would make corrections and send it back. Technology makes it much easier to remain an involved parent even when your child is not living under your roof.

Texting is a fabulous way for parents in high-conflict divorces to remain in contact with their children. The other parent often assumes the child is texting a friend or playing a game. Because children are adept at texting more than one person at once, they can text you without the other parent knowing. Make sure to "friend" your child on Facebook, use Instagram, and Twitter, and remember to use email to keep connected as well. Keep apprised of the new technologies children use and learn to use them too, so you can remain connected to your children when they are not with you.

It is also essential that your children have fun with you. Not that every day should be a party. Homework and household chores still need to be completed, but if the children enjoy being at your house they will want to stay. If, for example, you must rake the leaves, make it a family event. Shopping at Costco can be fun if you all stop for hotdogs and sodas after. Make your house the house the children want to bring their friends. Encourage them to have the sleepovers at your house and buy lots of popcorn and pizza. When it is time for homework, use that time to catch up on your own business. Then it becomes another "family time." Tell your children, "We'll all work for an hour, and then we will all take a break together." They are less likely to resist working if everyone is doing it together.

Fun is an essential ingredient to creating bonds between people, especially in trying times like during a divorce. If your children have fun with you, they will want to spend time with you. It is simple logic. Do not be concerned if you do not have much money. When you were a child, you were able to have fun without spending a lot of money. It is still possible. Every year on the day after Halloween, Camille spread out a picnic blanket on the floor and she and the kids ate their candy for dinner and their carrots for dessert. Joshua took his children to religious services every week. They were young and, by the time they were school age, it was such a staple in their lives that they enjoyed the time with their dad.

Maurice constantly complained that he did not have enough money to take his children out when they visited. He was angry because his ex-wife ridiculed him for his poverty, and he believed she was alienating the kids from him. He complained they were being "bought" by the expensive toys she gave them. It was difficult for Maurice to understand that by accepting her narrative, that he was poor, he was actually enabling his ex-wife's efforts to alienate him from his children. That is because Maurice allowed his situation to define him. I could see the bitterness in his demeanor and hear the anger in his voice. I am certain his children saw it, too. I am equally certain he was not successful at hiding his frustration when they were with him, that they felt uncomfortable and that their discomfort contributed to his sense of inadequacy. It became a self-fulfilling prophecy. No doubt the children stopped wanting to visit. It was not fun.

But there are plenty of things to do that do not cost a lot of money. Take the kids hiking, biking, swimming, and sledding. Attend art fairs and air shows. Maybe every Saturday night is movie night with popcorn and candy. Maybe you all read the Harry Potter series together. Maybe you all go ice skating or roller skating, or you buy a fifty-dollar fire pit and make s'mores. Be creative and be fun.

Creating fun traditions will help your children manage the conflict. Traditions will help your children feel a sense of stability. Fun traditions will make them want to participate. I have heard many parents complain about their ex-spouse being a "Disney Land" parent. The suggestion is that all the other parent does is play with the children while the complaining parent is left to "parent" the children. But if you allow yourself to be cast in the role of disciplinarian and you never deviate, then you have allowed your ex-spouse to write the narrative of your divorce. They are fun. You are sour.

You can still parent your children and raise them properly while being fun. The key is to respect your children. Respect is not based on rules. Every household should have rules. Respect is based on accepting a person's feelings, and if a parent fails to accept their child's feelings, then the child will not respect the parent. But if you acknowledge and respect the things that are important to your children, then they will acknowledge and respect the things that are important to you. By respecting your children's feelings, they understand they will always be accepted in your home and are less likely to want to leave, even if they are angry at you. Respect their feelings. Teach appropriate behavior. Provide structure. But make it fun.

Madison consistently disregarded her children's needs and wants. If the children needed to eat and she was still sleeping, the children went hungry. If the children wanted to go to gymnastics practice and she was at the computer, the children stayed home. The same type of behavior occurred at Gary's house. Yet both parents demanded obedience from their children and called it respect. Now, as teenagers, none of the children truly respect their other parents. Obedience is not respect. It is a power play where the adult always wins. No one, not even children, will remain in a relationship where they always lose or are always at the bottom of the power structure. Not when they have another parent who will accept their feelings and provide a fun and kid-centered home.

As for your ex-spouse's "Disney Land" activities, if your children are having fun then that is a good thing. Why shouldn't they have fun? And fun with the other parent will not impact your relationship with your children unless you let it. Your children are not so shallow to think that vacations are the only thing that matter in a relationship. If you are close to your children, accepting and loving, they will love you, too. Second, it is better for a Disney Land parent to remain a Disney Land parent than pretend to be a "real" parent. Allen's ex-wife sued him for custody of the children's homework. In her mind, she was an active parent, but every other weekend when the chil dren were with Allen, he found his ex-wife's copies of the homework. She never retrieved them from their sons' backpacks. This mother was not interested in parenting, and it would have been less costly and stressful had she acknowledged she was not really interested in her son's education and allowed Allen to manage that aspect of their sons' lives. A Disney Land parent who recognizes they are good at "fun" and that is all they want to do with their children is far less hostile than a parent who pretends otherwise. And there is nothing stopping you from being fun, too.

Acceptance of who your ex-spouse really is, and the parameters of your parenting plan is critical. You cannot control what happens in your ex-spouse's house any more than they can control what happens in your house. You have tools to manage the conflict and can elect to engage; but for many issues, you will need to simply let them go. When deciding, ask yourself if the problem is really yours or your ex-spouse's. If it is not your problem, then let it go. As soon as you try involving yourself or allowing your ex-spouse to involve you in a problem, you open the door for additional conflict. To the best of your ability, circumvent the other parent. Manage the situation yourself or with the aid of an outside party. Contact with your hostile ex-spouse should be kept to a minimum and center only on concrete issues, such as scheduling and logistics.

The most important thing to do is keep the dialogue open with your children. When your ex-spouse is making your children feel guilty for spending time with you or forbids them from speaking to you on their parenting time, talk to them about it. Ask your child how that makes them feel. Be the safe harbor, even if your children express love and loyalty to the parent who is hurting them. Acknowledging their loyalty to their other parent, acknowledges all of them, not just the parts you want to see. You can also help your children recognize the discomfort in their relationship with their other parent and help them problem-solve. If your son is complaining about something their father did, ask what he thinks could have been done differently. Help your child critically think so that they do not accept all their other parent's inappropriate behavior as "correct." Ask what you can do to help – short of intervening, of course. Being your children's safe harbor, no matter how much you hurt, will solidify, and preserve your relationship.

Never give up your parenting time. Doing so makes you complicit in your ex-spouse's efforts to alienate you from your children. Every moment you do not spend with your child is a lost opportunity to build the relationship and counteract your ex-spouse's attempts to alienate you. Even if your child is sick, bring them home and feed them chicken soup. Make sure they know you are there for them and have their back.

If you suspect your ex-spouse is undermining you by making subliminal suggestions such as, "Your dad isn't much fun, is he?"

or telling outright lies, spend a few minutes before the end of your parenting time debriefing. Review what you did together. Talk about what was fun. Acknowledge what did not go so well. Strategize how to make things better the next time. You may even go as far as to tell your children they are welcome to share their s experience with their other parent. You have no secrets. This small manipulation helps your child question whether "spying" is the right choice.

Ideally, you and your child can acknowledge your ex-spouse's alienation efforts by making private jokes about them. You can say, for example, "What happens at dad's house stays at dad's house," and then laugh and tell your children it is okay to share what happened at your house with their other parent. The key is to respect the dilemmas your children face. If you get angry, you only become an unwitting accomplice in your ex-spouse's alienation efforts.

Never forget that your children have a second home; if yours is too uncomfortable, they can ultimately choose not to see you. Technically, they cannot make this choice until they are eighteen, but if your 16-year-old son is six feet tall and weighs two hundred pounds, it will be difficult forcing them to remain with you. You must work from the beginning to make your children want to spend time with you. Make it fun. That does not mean you do not have rules. Children understand they need boundaries and consequences. But make your home child centered. Knowing that they are the most important part of your life will make them want to spend their time with you.

The most difficult lies to counteract are the lies with legal consequences. If your ex-spouse accuses you of molesting your child or creates false memories, you will need legal defense. But you will also have supervised visitation, which means you will have opportunities to speak to your child. Opening the dialogue will be difficult so do it in a way that makes your child feel safe. Have the supervisor sit with you while you ask your child questions such as: explain to me why you think this is true? Could there be any other explanation? Because I love you, I want you to have what you want — a relationship with your other parent. Why would I deny you that? I promise I do not hate your other parent more than I love you. It is widely believed among targeted parents that the strength and quality of their relationship with their child helped counteract the negative impact of any ongoing exposure to conflict.

If you feel your efforts are not effective enough, you may also want to consider employing a third-party parent coordinator to help you resolve these more difficult issues.

PARENT COORDINATORS

A parent coordinator is a mediator whose job is to resolve parenting issues outside the courtroom. They should be appointed by the court to require your ex-spouse to attend sessions. You cannot force them to participate, but they probably will since the parent coordinator reports back to the court.

The parenting coordinator can be a jack-of-all-trades. They might serve as mediator, arbitrator, coach, counselor, and court liaison. Their job:

- ❖ Monitoring and facilitating the implementation of the par-
- ❖ Modifying the plan to promote non-conflicting implementation.
- ❖ Helping parents promote and encourage positive relationships between the child and the other parent.

- ❖ Facilitating referrals for psychological or other help a parent or the child exhibits the need for.
- ❖ Providing educational guidance on child development.
- ❖ Making recommendations to the court in cases of impasse.
- ❖ Working within the scope, defined by the court, in making decisions for the parties regarding child-related issues.

Approach meetings with your parent coordinator in the same manner as you approached mediation. You must prepare. Research your coordinator (most will have Web pages). Learn their style. If your coordinator prefers tackling smaller issues first to achieve success and establish a framework for success, then come to the meeting prepared to relent on one of those minor issues. This will make you appear conciliatory and reasonable and will also embolden your coordinator. If your coordinator prefers diving into the big issues straight away, be ready with your explanation of why your position is in your child's best interests. You must also be prepared to respond to your ex-spouse's major arguments. You will already know them because by the time you reach the point of needing the parent coordinator's help, you and your ex-spouse will have been arguing over the issue for some time.

Your parent coordinator will try to remain neutral. That means they will not always agree with you. If you feel strongly enough about an issue, you can always use your tool of last resort – court.

TEACHING YOUR CHILDREN TO ADVOCATE

In a high-conflict case, it is necessary to teach your older children strategies for coping with their other parent. To grow up healthy, your children must be able to recognize and cope with inappropriate parental behavior. If your ex-spouse allows their new spouse to bully your children, teach them how to navigate life in that household. Teach them when to engage, when not to engage, and how to successfully engage if they must do so. Having lived with your ex-spouse, you know and understand their deficiencies. It is likely that as your children grow older, they will confront those same deficiencies. Validate their experiences. It is not disparaging to commiserate with your children and say that you have had similar experiences when you lived with their other parent. It is the truth. Do not insult your ex-spouse. Do not call them names. But if you fail to acknowledge that their behavior was inappropriate, you are enabling them as if you never divorced. By acknowledging that your ex-spouse's behavior was improper, you are providing your children with an alternative point of view. Be prepared, however, for the day they tell you that your experiences are not their experiences. It is true, and if your child is telling you this it is because they no longer want your advice, so know that it is time to stop. But still be available to help when they encounter difficult situations involving other people. If your child has a problem with a teacher or a boss, be ready to help them problem-solve. By helping your children develop coping strategies, you are helping them adjust not just to the divorce, but also to life.

You do your children an enormous disservice if you pretend that inappropriate behavior is acceptable. But do not fall into the trap of agreeing that everything your ex-spouse does is incorrect. If your ex-spouse punished your child for failing to clean their room and your child complains to you, you can support your ex-spouse. This teaches your children that people are complex and even their disordered parent has good sides to their personality.

While you cannot stop your ex-spouse from creating situations that are inherently illogical and uncomfortable for your children, (unless the situation is illegal or highly unsafe), you can help by teaching them to advocate for themselves. Madison once told her older daughter that if she did not wear a wrist guard (which embarrassed the teenage girl) to her younger sister's roller-skating party, *she* (the daughter) would be responsible for forcing Madison to cancel the party. The girl did not understand why this reasoning was illogical, but it felt wrong. She called her father for a "reality check" and he helped her find the words to explain and differentiate between reasonable and unreasonable rules. This strategy session helped immensely. The teenager was able to advocate for herself and eventually Madison relented. The party took place without the teenager having to wear the embarrassing wrist guards.

Teaching your children to advocate for themselves will help them get their reasonable demands met. Donna's son desperately wanted to go to overnight summer camp but was prevented by his father who claimed to love him so much that he (dad) could not bear to be apart from him. After Donna and her son practiced "negotiating," he was able to offer his father more time together in exchange for camp. When his father called to verify this and learned that Donna was willing to give up proportionally more of her summertime with their son than he would be giving up, dad finally agreed. Donna's son learned valuable negotiating skills. He also learned that his father's argument was not as much about wanting to spend time together but about wanting to gain an advantage over his mother He learned to differentiate words from actions.

As your children begin to distinguish words and actions, they will likely call or text you for that reality check. They will call and say, "Mom did this" or "Dad did that." What they are really looking for is validation that the actions hurt. By validating their truth and then helping them understand why their other parent's actions do not conform to the words, you help your children navigate their relationship with that parent. Eventually, they will no longer be convinced that the words "I love you" mean they must subordinate themselves to everything that parent demands. Eventually, they will learn to steer the conversation away from words of love to words of problem solving. "I want to go to camp. How can we make that happen?" should become your children's mantra. The answer, "I love you," eventually begins to sound lame. Teach your children to hold out. The subliminal message: "If you really love me, you'll agree to my reasonable requests." Eventually, that parent must respond with words other than words of love. Either they begin to negotiate, or they reach an impasse. If that conversation ends in an impasse, then your children have learned that sad but valuable lesson, which is that their other parents' words of love are just that – words.

Your children help themselves by learning to advocate for themselves. Patricia refused to allow her son to play hockey. She had read that a child had been killed by a hockey puck and did not want her son playing. Yet the boy loved hockey and longed to join the team with his friends. The more she refused, the more he wanted it. Patricia's ex-husband did not have enough parenting time to enroll the child in hockey himself, but he did enroll the child in weeklong hockey camps during school and summer holidays. He also hosted a skating party for his son's birthday. The more the boy played, the more he advocated for himself, and the more difficult it became for Patricia to deny him. Eventually, she relented.

Patricia's ex-husband understood that if he engaged Patricia directly, she would never relent. But this father listened to his son's reasonable requests and collaborated with his son to achieve his goal, despite the obstructions Patricia presented. This father also taught his son how to advocate for himself. Learning to advocate is a skill every person can use. Your children cannot get everything they want and teaching them to advocate includes teaching them reasonable expectations. But it also includes teaching them to problem-solve. Patricia's son learned that his mother was being overly cautious and, by demonstrating that the risks were smaller than she perceived, he learned how to address her concerns. Not by words, but by actions. By playing hockey during his father's parenting time, Patricia's son taught her that he could play safely.

By collaborating with his son to help him achieve his goals, father and son grew closer. The boy understood that his father had *heard* him and was championing his cause. In that high-conflict case, the father had no influence over his ex-wife, but the son did. Despite her psychological issues, Patricia loved (or believed she loved) her son and, therefore, he had "leverage." He could advocate for himself because his mother was more likely to listen to him than to her ex-husband.

You and your child are bound by the parenting plan until they become an adult. Eighteen is the legal magic number, but sixteen is the practical magic number. Save your pennies to buy your teenage child a car. Once that child is mobile, they can drive themself and their younger siblings to their other parent's home for parenting time. They can also *leave*. Teach your child that the car keys belong to you, and their other parent has no legal right to take them away. If your child is punished frequently for leaving or trying to leave, add that to your pile of evidence that their other parent is trying to stifle the child's natural and age-appropriate developmental stage of growing independence.

Remember that by the time your children are teenagers, they are likely to have formed strong opinions about their parents. Many choose not to see the offending parent, and many narcissistic parents have difficulty accepting that. So as your children grow older and your ex-spouse demands to see them, be agreeable. Respond by saying, "Sure, give Bobby a call on his cell phone," knowing that your ex-spouse may not call because they cannot face the rejection. This is when you have two conversations. The "conversation" with your ex-spouse – always through email – confirms that they can collect the child at the designated time. The conversation with your child is about strategies. If your child does not want to spend time with their other parent but is required by court order to do so, then the strategy to teach him is to keep busy. Encourage them to spend time studying because school is a legitimate barrier to an overbearing adult. Your children should also get involved in extracurricular activities, preferably school-related activities. Teach your children at an early age how to make play dates so when they become teenagers, they have the skills necessary for arranging sleepovers and other activities that will fill their time. The more time at these activities, the less time is spent with the parent who is making them miserable. You can always send your ex-spouse an email saying something like: "Just learned that Joe has a practice after school. He will be ready at six." Not only have you helped your child feel more in control of their schedule, but you are also helping them gain the benefits of being involved. Second, evidence that your children's other parent is preventing them from participating in school events is powerful evidence that the parent is not acting in the children's best interests.

Another strategy is to role-play with your children. Anticipate how their other parent will respond when they assert their independence, and then brainstorm responses. Encourage your children to memorize "answers" to likely arguments.

Third, tell your children that if they ever feel unsafe or feel the need to leave their other parent's home, they should call you. You cannot pick them up from their other parent's house, but once they have left you *can* ensure their safety. You will have to return them, but when a child leaves their other parent's house, it produces more evidence that things are not going well there. If your ex-spouse lives far away, then when your children are old enough, make sure they have a credit card and talk about how to call an Uber, and about safety.

If you fear that your children may be physically threatened, enroll them in a martial arts or self-defense class. Help them gain the confidence to know they can defend themselves if necessary. Other things to do if you are concerned about your child's physical safety:

❖ Teach your young child how to dial 911 if they feel threatened.

❖ Teach your child a code word to use in case they need you to call the police to rescue them.

Make sure your child memorizes your work telephone number and your parents' number so they can verify the truth if told that you are too sick for them to return to you, or worse, that you are dead.

While we never want our children to be hurt, especially by their other parent, if your children need to use any of these strategies, then fortunately or unfortunately, you have evidence of a change in circumstances that gives grounds for a change in the custody or parenting plan.

By teaching your children to look beyond words and rationalizations to discern the true intent of rules and conditions, you are teaching them invaluable critical-thinking skills. By teaching your children to differentiate words and actions, and by teaching them to listen to those feelings in the pit of their stomach, you may be helping them make better choices than you did. Not only will you rescue your children from years of therapy, but you also may prevent them from marrying someone with similar behavior patterns as your ex-spouse. And by validating their feelings, you are teaching your children to trust themselves and know that that they will always have a safe haven with you.

In addition to you, your children have another powerful ally: their siblings. In a divorced family, the sibling relationship is the most important relationship in the children's lives. That is because there is no other person on Earth who understands what it is like to live in both your house and your ex-spouse's home. No other person will ever share the unique experience of living in these two households. And, therefore, only a sibling can ever truly validate your child's experiences.

Teach your children to value their siblings above all others. If so, they will always have allies and other people who can conduct a "reality check" with them. By having fun together, your children bond. Encourage them to bond further by attending one another's events and supporting each other. Make certain younger Billy attends older sister Tracy's dance recital and that she cheers him on at his lacrosse game. Explain that they need to support one another – and hope this lesson lasts a lifetime.

It is helpful to have regular strategy sessions. When your children are having difficulty resolving an issue with a friend, teacher, or another person in their life, brainstorm solutions together. Include the entire family and do not censor any idea until they are all on the table and the pros and cons are dissected. By participating in problem solving, children learn that every problem has a solution and that they should not feel defeated. They learn that if Plan A does not work, there is always Plan B. These strategy sessions can also create a bonding experience because the family is working together. It may feel like it is your family against the world, but at least the family is together.

SELF-HELP

There will be times, of course, when you will need to act. Self-help is when you take matters into your own hands without first seeking court approval. If you chose this route, know that you will sometimes win and you will sometimes lose. Even if you win, however, there will always be a price to pay. That is, you anger the judge in your case.

Dan had been trying to modify his parenting plan but had not been successful. Dan's ex-wife's attorney had aggressively kept him out of court, even going as far as failing to inform Dan about a change in a hearing date. His ex-wife's victories had empowered her, and she was increasingly flaunting the terms of the parenting plan. Dan became concerned she would kidnap the children. She had lost her house and her job and had asked for the children's passports. After asking for reassurance and receiving none, Dan made the unilateral decision not to allow her to take the children during a vacation. The result was as he predicted. She immediately filed a motion for contempt against him. While Dan was ordered to pay a small fine and give up some of his parenting time to replace the time his ex-wife lost, he felt it was a worthwhile price because he was finally able to get his issues before the court.

David was angry because his ex-wife was leaving the country for 10 days and refused to allow the children to be with him. Instead, she insisted that the children, who were teenagers, remain with her husband. David asked several times for the children to be with him while she was gone because he knew they disliked their stepfather and preferred staying with him. Instead of securing an order from the court when the mother flew out of the country, David offered the children the opportunity to come home with him. They chose to do so. David then sent his ex-wife and her husband an email telling them that the children were with him, that they were safe and that he would return them to their mother as soon as she returned home. David kept his word, but that did not stop his ex-wife from filing a complaint against him.

This strategy backfired on her, however, when the ex-wife lied in court and claimed she had left a power of attorney with her husband. Recognizing that David had joint legal custody, the court ruled against the ex-wife because she had denied David his legal rights. Self-help then, can be a win or lose prospect. There is always a cost.

David had to pay several thousand dollars in attorney fees to defend himself. Dan had to pay a fine to the court. But for each of them, the money was worth the gain.

BLENDING YOUR NEW FAMILY

Your remarriage may set off an entirely new round of conflict with your ex-spouse. The new parent figure in your children's lives may ignite your ex-spouse's anger. Their anger may be caused because you were not supposed to move on, marry, and be happy. It might be because you chose someone over them – even though they rejected you by divorcing you. Any number of reasons can spark your ex-spouse's outrage, resulting in harassment, enhanced efforts to control you or the children, or more litigation. On top of this disruption to your happiness, you may have new stepchildren who are adjusting to your place in *their* lives. It is a challenging time.

You and your new spouse should establish fun traditions with your new family. The first year should be filled with field trips whenever the family is together. If children have different interests, rotate so that each event caters to one child, explaining that everyone will have a turn. Find something everybody likes to do. Again, the key is to make it fun for the kids to be together so that they want to be with you.

This strategy may cause the unwanted side effect of inflaming your ex-spouse. Accept that it does hurt to be excluded from the fun your children are having, but regardless, your ex-spouse may not sabotage your new family bonding. Whatever crisis or activity your ex-spouse invents to distract you from focusing on your new family, remember that you do not need to respond. Their problem need not become your problem. During that first year of marriage, there is nothing more important than blending your new family.

As a new stepparent, you cannot replace a child's biological parent no matter how awful you believe that person is. But you can be the kindly aunt or uncle, the big brother or sister, the wise older friend. Your role in their life at the beginning is to be a *host*, as if the kids were at your house on an old-fashioned play date. And your agenda is to develop that aunt/uncle, big brother/big sister relationship, so they come to you for advice and support.

If your stepchild does approach you with reasonable complaints about their biological parent, try being very matter of fact about things. Listen. Sympathize with their feelings. Help them problem solve. That is, help them find a way to achieve their reasonable wishes despite the obstacle that is their biological parent. And suggest that you believe their biological parent loves them, but that they make different parenting choices than you do. This approach makes the other parent accessible, even if they are hurting the child, and prevents the child from feeling bad for loving that other parent. More importantly, it makes you another safe harbor for the child.

Having a new stepparent is difficult for children and it takes time for them to grow comfortable with a new person in their life. Encourage all the children to talk to one another about what life is like in your house. Accept your stepchildren's feelings as you accept your own children's, even if their feelings are anger toward you. A child's feelings are always okay. A child's bad behavior is not.

Establish rules in your house and make punishments be the logical consequence of the infraction. Make the rules simple, such as, "In this house, we respect one another." If there is respect, Gillian will not borrow Jamie's clothes without asking, and Bobbie will not interrupt. By selecting a few simple rules with wide-ranging applications, your new stepchildren will not feel that their new home is too strict. At first, it is better to allow your new spouse to discipline your stepchildren but allow those children to understand that you were part of the decision-making process. Make certain the punishments are reasonable and explain to the children what would have been a better choice. It does no good to punish children for the wrong choice if they do not understand what would have been appropriate. It is a challenge to build a blended family while learning to live with a new spouse. Make certain to have a date night. Be available to go out with your couple-friends. But do not go out *only* when his kids are with their mom, or her kids are with their dad. Alternate your nights out so that no group of siblings feels they are less important because you are not there when they are home alone.

Be patient. Everything takes longer to adjust to than you would expect or hope for. In the meantime, even though your ex-spouse may be on the warpath, know that it is because you have found happiness and that was not in their game plan.

WINNING YOUR
HIGH-CONFLICT DIVORCE

For me, winning my high-conflict divorce meant knowing that my children and I are happy with the quality of our lives and the family we have built. Your win, your happiness, is in your future, too. The key is not to let your high-conflict divorce define you. Know that it is only a part of your story and that, one day, this part of your story will be over, and a new part of your story will begin. Remember that life is change. There is an old parable about King Solomon, who once confessed to his advisers that he felt depressed. When things were going well, he feared they would end. When things were going badly, he feared they would not end. King Solomon finally achieved peace of mind when presented with a ring upon which were engraved the words: "This, too, shall pass." Your high-conflict divorce shall pass, too.

The strategies in this book will help. At each step along the way, do your best to remain mindful and have a plan. I had a client facing a custody trial. He had a fifty percent chance of winning. While he went to court prepared to win, he also went prepared to lose. Knowing his ex-wife also faced a fifty percent chance of losing, he was ready in case she offered to settle "on the courthouse steps" – that is, if she asked to negotiate just before the trial was set to begin. My client went to court armed with two parenting plans – one for the judge and one to use for negotiations. The second parenting plan contained compromises he was willing to live with. Embedded in it were also negotiable demands – things he would ask for but knew he could give up in exchange for something else. In this way, my client took control of his conflict. He would not get everything he wanted, but by preparing for both possibilities – winning or losing – he increased his chances of getting much of what he wanted. And that was his win, remaining in control of the process.

Once you have identified your long-term goals, always keep them "in your back pocket." That is, whenever a conflict arises, chose a response that will help you achieve that distant goal. Sometimes, no matter how painful, giving in might be the right response. Sometimes you may need to fight. But your "pocket" should never be empty. It should always hold your short- and long-term goals, as well as the many tools at your disposal to manage your interactions with your ex-spouse. It should also contain a copy of all your court orders.

Know that there *is* a solution to every problem. Never stop believing that. The answer may take a while to discover: It might be Plan D (after having tried Plans A, B and C), but it *will* present itself. Even if you lose a battle, there is usually a way to turn some of your loss into a win. It just may take more time.

And finally, never forget what *your* "win" looks like. Your "win" might be a new family. It might be a new spouse. It might be you and your children living alone together without interference from your ex-spouse. It might be a whole new career. Or a completely different life adventure. But wherever you go with your life, you do not need your ex-spouse holding you back. Your "win" will be moving happily on with your new life.

REFERENCES

American Bar Association. Domestic Violence Statistics. Available from: http://www.americanbar.org/groups/domestic_violence/resources/statistics.html#teens (30 July 2014).

Baerger, D., Galatzer-Levy, R., Gould, J. & Nye, J. & Sandra, G. (2002). A methodology for reviewing the reliability and relevance of child custody evaluations. *Journal of the American Academy of Matrimonial Lawyers.* 18, 35-589.

Baker, A. & Darnall, D. (2006). Behaviors and strategies employed in parental alienation. *Journal of Divorce & Remarriage.* 45:1-2, 97-124.

Baum, N. & Shnit, D. (2005). Self-differentiation and narcissism in divorced parents' co-parental relationships and functioning. *Journal of Divorce & Remarriage.* 42:3-43:3-60.

Beyer, E. (2008). Comment: a pragmatic look at mediation and collaborative law as alternatives to family law litigation. *St. Mary's L. J.* 40: 303.

Bokker P. (2006) Factors that influence the relationships between divorced fathers and their children. *Journal of Divorce & Remarriage.* 45:3-4, 157-172.

Bonach, K. (2005). Factors contributing to quality co-parenting. *Journal of Divorce & Remarriage.* 43:3-4, 79-103.

Dalton, C, Drozd, L. & Wong, F. Navigating Custody and Visitation Evaluations in Cases with Domestic Violence: A Judge's Guide. Available from http://www.afccnet.org/Portals/0/PublicDocuments/ProfessionalResources/BenchGuide.pdf (30 July 2014).

Diagnostic and statistical manual of mental disorders: DSM-5. (5th ed.). (2013). Washington, D.C.: American Psychiatric Association.

Diagnostic and statistical manual of mental disorders: DSM-IV-TR. (4th ed.). (2000). Washington, DC: American Psychiatric Association.

Domestic Violence Resource Center. Available from: http://dvrc-or.org/domestic/violence/resources/C61/. (28 October 2013).

Douglas, E. (2003). The impact of a presumption for joint legal custody on father involvement. *Journal of Divorce & Remarriage.* 39:1-2,1-10.

Dreman, S. (2000). The influence of divorce on children. *Journal of Divorce & Remarriage.* 32:3-4, 41-71.

Eisenstat, S. & Bancroft, L. (1999). Domestic violence. *The New England Journal of Medicine.* 341.12, 886-892.

Fischer, R. (1998). The impact of an educational seminar for divorcing parents. *Journal of Divorce & Remarriage.* 28:1-2, 35-48.

Elrod, L. (2001). A Minnesota comparative family law symposium: reforming the system to protect children in high-conflict custody cases. *Wm. Mitchell L. Rev.*28: 495.

Finlay v. Finlay, 240 N.Y. 429, 148 N.E. 624 (N.Y. 1925).

Gilmore, S. (2006). Contact/shared residence and child well-being: research evidence and its implications for legal decision making. *International Journal of Law, Policy, and the Family.* 20, 344-365.

Haas, T. (2004). Child custody determinations in Michigan: not in the best interests of children and parents. *University of Detroit Law Review.* 81:3.

Henry, W., Fieldstone, L., Thompson, M. & Treharne, K. (2011). Parenting coordination as an antidote for high-conflict divorce and court re-litigation. *Journal of Divorce & Remarriage.* 52:7, 455-471.

Hutchinson, E. *Dimensions of human behavior.* (2003). London: Sage Publications.

In re Parentage of L.B. (2005) 155 Wash.2d 679, 122 P.3d 161, cert. denied, 126 S. Ct. 2021, 547 U.S. 1143, 164 L.Ed.2d 806.

Jellinek, M, Erwin, K., & Bagnell, A. (2000). Contentious divorce: the rocky path to the child's best interests. *U. Ark. Little Rock L. Rev.* 22: 375.

Jones, T. & Bodtker, A. (1999). Agreement, maintenance, satisfaction, and re-litigation in mediated and non-mediated custody cases. *Journal of Divorce & Remarriage*.a32:1-2, 17-30.

Kot L. & Shoemaker, H. (1999). Children of divorce. *Journal of Divorce & Remarriage*. 31:1-2, 161-178.

Lachkar, J. (1986). Narcissistic borderline couples: implications for mediation. *Conciliation Courts Review*. 24: 1, 31.

Langenbrunner, M., Cox, M. & Cherry, D. (2013). Psychometrics of LOCA: level of conflict assessment of divorcing or separating couples. *Journal of Divorce & Remarriage*. 54:6, 439-457.

Linehan, M. (1993). *Skills training manual for treating borderline personality disorder*. The Guildford Press: New York.

Lyon. (2009). Narcissism Epidemic: Why There Are So Many Narcissists Now. *U.S. News and World Report*. Available from: http://health.usnews.com/health-news/family-health/brain-and-behavior/articles/2009/04/21/narcissism-epidemic-why-there-are-so-many-narcissists-now. (31 July 31, 2013).

Macie, K. & Stolberg, A. (2003). Assessing parenting after divorce. *Journal of Divorce & Remarriage*. 39:1-2, 89-107.

Malcore, S., Windell, J., Seyuin, M. & Hill, E. (2009) Predictors of continued conflict after divorce or separation: evidence from a high-conflict group treatment program. *Journal of Divorce & Remarriage.* 51:1, 50-64.

National Coalition against Domestic Violence. Domestic Violence Facts. Available from: http://www.ncadv.org/files/DomesticViole nceFactSheet%28National%29.pdf. (28 October 28, 2013).

National Institute of Health. Facts for Families, American Academy of Child & Adolescent Psychiatry. 1: 10/92. Available from: www. NIH.Gov/MedlinePluse/Divorce. (9 January 2010).

National Institute of Mental Health. Statistics. Available from: http://www.nimh.nih.gov/health/publications/the-numbers-count-mental-disorders-in-america/index.shtml. (5 August 2013).

Neal, R. The Divorce Process. Available from: http://www.cbsnews. com/2100-500168_162-528027.html. (11 February 2009).

Neff, R. & Cooper, K. (2004). Parental conflict resolution six-, twelve, and fifteen-month follow-ups of a high-conflict program. *Family Court Review.* 42: 99.

Nichols, M. (2009). *The essentials of family therapy*, (4th ed.). Pearson: Boston.

Nielsen, L. (2011). Shared parenting after divorce: a review of shared residential parenting research. *Journal of Divorce & Remarriage*. 52:8, 586-609.

Oakland County Michigan ADEPT (after divorce: effective parenting techniques) Program. Available from: http://www.oakgov.com/courts/circuit/Pages/program_service/adept.aspxhttp://www.oakgov.com/courts/circuit/Pages/program_service/adept.aspx. (22 January 2009).

Payson, E. (2002). *The wizard of Oz and other narcissists: coping with the one-way relationship in work, love, and family*. Royal Oak, Mich.: Julian Day Publications.

Portes, P., Lehman, A. & Brown, J. (1999). The child adjustment inventory. *Journal of Divorce & Remarriage*. 30:1-2, 37-45.

Pruett, M. K., Hoganbruen, K & Jackson, T. (2000). The best interest of the child. *Journal of Divorce & Remarriage*. 33:1-2, 47-63.

Robertson, L. (2013). The experience of parental conflict in parallel parenting custody arrangements. University of Saskatchewan. Available from: http://ecommons.usask.ca/bitstream/handle/10388/ETD-2012-12-930/ROBERTSON-DISSERTATION.pdf?sequence=5. (30 July 2014).

Sanders, J. (2007). Age-appropriate parenting plans: child development information. *American Journal of Family Law*. 67.

Sarrazin, J. & Cyr, F. (2007). Parental conflicts and their damaging effects on children. *Journal of Divorce & Remarriage.* 47:1-2, 77-93.

Schum, L. & Stolberg, A. (2007). Standardization of the co-parenting behavior questionnaire. *Journal of Divorce & Remarriage.* 47:3-4, 103-132.

Singer, M. (1998). The mental health consequences of children's exposure to violence. *Cuyahoga County Community Health Research Institute, Mandel School of Applied Social Sciences,* Case Western Reserve University. (28 October 2013).

Stamps, L. (2002). Maternal preference in child custody decisions. *Journal of Divorce & Remarriage.* 37:1-2, 1-11.

Sullivan, M. (2008). Parenting coordination: coming of age? *Family Court Review.* 51: 56.

United States Department of Justice. Domestic Violence. Available from: http://www.ovw.usdoj.gov/domviolence.htm. (28 October 28, 2013).

Vecchi, G., (2009). Conflict & crisis communication: methods of crisis intervention and stress management. *Annals of the American Psychotherapy Association.* 12:4, 54.

Weinstein, J. & Weinstein, R. (2005) "I know better than that:" the role of emotions and the brain. *J. L. Fam. Stud.* 7: 351.

Willemsen, E., Andrews, R, Karlin, B. & Willemsen, M. (2005). The Ethics of the child custody process: are the American Law Institute's guidelines the answer? *Child & Adolescent Social Work Journal.* 22:2.

Zorza, J., (2009). Domestic violence report & sexual assault report. *Washington, DC, Journal of Child Custody.* 6, 258.